The Rebirth
of God and Lisa

JEAN-JACQUES TRIFAULT

The Rebirth of God and Lisa

Jean-Jacques Trifault

Footsteps to Wisdom Publishing

THE REBIRTH OF GOD AND LISA
Jean-Jacques Trifault

Footsteps to Wisdom Publishing

Copyright (C)2005 by Jean-Jacques Trifault
Second Edition 2015

Cover illustration, "Rainbow God" by Michael Partis

TABLE OF CONTENTS

INTRODUCTION	 7
FIRST MEETING A Place Where God Can Meet Us	 9
SECOND MEETING Nothing Happens by Accident	 28
THIRD MEETING Freedom from Guilt	 42
FOURTH MEETING An Awareness of God	 56
FIFTH MEETING A Lovely Relationship	 77
SIXTH MEETING The Ripening Fruit	 93
SEVENTH MEETING A Receptor for Love	 124
EIGHTH MEETING Will the Seed Develop?	 145
NINTH MEETING A Mother's Love	 167
TENTH MEETING God's Daughter	 178
ELEVENTH MEETING We are Reborn	 195
TWELFTH MEETING Notes from Lisa	 215

INTRODUCTION

My name is Lisa, and the book you are holding is an account of several extraordinary meetings I experienced.

At the time my story began, I was living by myself in an apartment and had a job I liked that kept me quite busy. I had moved to a city from a smaller town, searching for opportunities to pursue my dream of becoming successful.

Some mornings I went to the gym before work, and after a full day at my job, I took evening classes two nights a week to further my career. I had moved up to the position of manager, and was hoping eventually to advance further.

On weekends I spent time with friends, walking around the city, shopping, exploring, and maybe visiting a museum or a park. Then after eating at a favorite restaurant, we might go to see a movie.

Everything was going quite smoothly at my job and in my life in general, and I felt confident I could handle whatever challenge might come up. At some point, however, I started to experience feelings of loneliness inside myself. Sometimes in quiet moments questions started coming to my mind. Was life's only purpose to have a good career and a comfortable lifestyle? Even though my life was going in that direction, something in me didn't feel fulfilled.

At times I found myself thinking about some kind of God. Did He really exist? I even tried to talk to Him a few times, regardless I didn't know how. Growing up I had gone to church but had *eventually grown disinterested and even began to look down on people who were religious, feeling they were naïve or unrealistic.*

Then one Saturday morning, something happened while I was sitting at my table, drinking a cup of tea and preparing to write a few sentences in my journal. My mind had started wandering when all of a sudden a clear, soft voice emerged through my drifting thoughts, greeting me. I was taken by surprise, but the voice continued. Incredibly, it was God who was speaking to me!

The following account explains how everything unfolded, based upon my notes and from my memory. To say that this event had a huge effect upon my life is an understatement.

FIRST MEETING

 ## The Rebirth of God and Lisa

God: Good morning, Lisa!

Lisa: Oh, is there someone there?! Who are you?

God: It is your God who is speaking, Lisa.

Lisa: Really!? It can't be! You can speak to me, here, just like this?

God: Well, Lisa, you have tried to speak to Me several times, in several different places. So today, when I saw you here, at your sunny table with your writing paper, I felt invited to speak to you.

Lisa: I feel shocked! Even though I have tried to speak to You recently, I didn't really expect to get a response. I don't really know how to react, or even what to call You.

God: Well, just to welcome Me would be a good start. Concerning My name, I do not have a specific name to give to you. Whatever you want to call Me is fine. The most important thing is to realize you are speaking to Me.

Lisa: Oh, maybe I'm having a dream. But I'm pretty sure I'm wide awake, and everything else seems normal.

God: Yes, Lisa, everything is 'normal', if you wish to use that word. I am waiting for you to become calm again.

Lisa: Actually, earlier today I did feel unusually calm. I was a bit surprised, because my mind is usually so occupied. And it was at that point that I started thinking about You.

First meeting

God: Yes, I could perceive your calmness. It is one of the reasons I could come to you. Another reason is that you chose to think about Me. Thinking about Me opened something inside of you and I could approach you, regardless it was just a small amount of space.

Lisa: Oh, I had no idea that's how it works! I would think You could approach people whenever You liked.

God: If you are busy with many thoughts, there is no room for Me to approach you, regardless of the power you believe I have.

Lisa: It's true, there is often a lot going on in my mind. But I would never have imagined my thoughts could stop You from coming to speak to me.

God: Your thoughts are for Me like noise is for you in your world. When there is too much noise, you cannot hear your mind. So, when you think too much—and it looks like you think a lot, by the way, though I am not sure about what—your thoughts create so many waves, or so much noise. Therefore it is impossible for Me to talk to you or for you to hear Me.

Lisa: I do have a tendency to think about many things. Sometimes I initiate a thought consciously, and sometimes I just start thinking about things without really knowing why.

God: Maybe you learned to think when you were going to school. Then after a while it came to a point where you couldn't stop thinking, even if you tried. What do you have to say about that?

Lisa: That is possible. When we attend school, it is very unpopular to be quiet and to not have any opinions. If someone were to ask me, "What are you thinking?" and I were to answer, "Nothing," people would think I am strange.

God: Oh, it seems you want to be sincere with Me. I like that. And, it looks like you really know yourself, don't you?

Lisa: Yes, I guess so. I've lived with myself for quite a long time. Actually, I'm still trying to accept the way I am. But I never realized that when I'm thinking too much, it can be an obstacle for You to approach me.

God: Yes, all those thoughts are an obstacle for Me to come. They create such a blockage that I cannot initiate any idea inside your mind or inside your conscience, and therefore I cannot help you to direct yourself in the way I think you should go. Would you like for Me to direct you?

Lisa: Direct me? I'm not really sure what to think about that. Would that mean that I might have to change some of the things I do?

God: Is that a bad idea?

Lisa: Perhaps not. I do have some habits that for some reason I don't really feel good about. For example, when I come home from work, my plan is to first relax, but I find myself running from one thing to another. I turn on some music and look through my mail. Then I check my messages and at the same time I go to the kitchen and make a snack. As I'm eating I turn on the TV and flip through the channels, and so forth.
    This is what I do most evenings without thinking too much

First meeting

about it, but I wonder if this pattern blocks You from coming.

God: I am not so sure what you are doing everyday, because for Me you are moving too fast to the point I cannot catch your wavelength. Added to that, there is no space for Me to come inside you, because your mind is too occupied. Overall, you demonstrate that I am not a part of your life, because you do not think about Me or mention My name.

But what is interesting to Me is that in spite of My difficulty to approach human beings, many of them can still believe I am with them.

Lisa: I have heard people speaking about You, and some said that they felt You were with them. I wondered how they could say that.

God: Yes, many people claim that I am with or among them. People like to welcome this idea. However, it makes Me somehow laugh that these people believe that I am always waiting, I guess on top of their roof, for the moment when they think about Me or call Me. They hope I will instantaneously appear, like a magical event.

Lisa: Although I did not have the concept that You could be somewhere close to me, I liked to believe in the possibility that You existed.

God: I am very pleased that You accepted to recognize some possibility for My existence. But I think to believe that I can live around you is also good. I say this because people who believe I live around them have the wish to find Me within a deep part of themselves. Yet their mistake is to believe I am always there waiting for their commands and requests. I think they would be shocked if they knew the reality and understood My difficulty to come close to them.

Lisa: Well, maybe You're not totally aware of the reality here. Basically, we only think about our own situations. It seems to me that people only call You when they face some problem, hoping You will come to fix whatever they struggle with.

God: Yes, many times I am expected to be like a city agency, ready to pick up the phone and solve any problem or emergency, similar to your firemen or paramedics, who basically are always waiting to be called. People do not know that this is not My purpose. As well, I cannot fix situations involving physical matter as fast as you can, regardless of the fact that many people believe I can do anything I want.

Lisa: I once met a person who was angry with You. Actually this person was a friend of mine. When I asked her, "Why are you so angry, what happened to you?" she answered, "God didn't help me when I needed Him." She said that some time ago she had wanted to get a specific job, thinking it would make her really happy. She prayed to You, hoping You would assist her. After she went to the interview the manager didn't hire her and she accused You of not helping her.

I was so surprised at that time. But now that You speak about people's expectations of You, I understand what happened.

God: After hearing this example, I can say that you at least do not demonstrate this kind of behavior. Maybe it is because you do not really believe in Me or maybe just because you do not have the concept that I should do something for you. Either way, I do appreciate it.

First meeting

Still I can tell you, even if I have the desire to meet you, you block Me by having so much conversation going on inside your mind and by your tendency to argue with what is happening in your life.

Lisa: I feel a little bit strange to talk back to You, but I see things a bit differently. Yes, it is true I have plenty of wishes coming from all different parts of me, but I believe this is something good, because these desires help me to challenge myself to accomplish bigger things, even to the point where I get a bit insistent if people don't agree with me. But I certainly don't think about accusing You every time something doesn't go the way I like.

God: I am very pleased you don't accuse Me for the difficulties you have in fulfilling your wishes. By not accusing Me, I can at least feel I can approach you.

Lisa: Well, I'm certainly very happy that You could come. At the same time I'm not sure of what I should do with this conversation, not in regards to me but if I think about telling other people. At least I will try to write down what You tell me, so I'm sure to remember everything.

God: I think if you write everything down, it is wonderful for Me and I believe for you too, because after this moment together you can review all your notes and this can make a base for Me to meet you again.

Lisa: Can I tell You something?

God: Yes, you can tell Me something. But it sounds very serious. It seems I need to change My attitude to listen to you, that I must really concentrate now.

Lisa: It's about all these thoughts I have. Sometimes I want to fulfill something more profound and meaningful than what I have been doing so far. Other times my thoughts focus on advancing my career and becoming better off. These desires are so strong in me, pulling me in different directions, to the point where I feel split or divided. I don't know if this is good.

God: I didn't know you had this kind of situation. Very few people mention to Me that they struggle with this. Most of them experience either one or the other side of this kind of desire. Either they wish to fulfill every dream of the material world, or they only want to focus on their spiritual life.

It looks like you have discovered a new reality in yourself. It will not be easy to satisfy both sides at the same time.

Lisa: You know, very recently I had yet another thought. It happened when I was walking around in the park the other day, which I enjoy to do very much. I saw a little girl who lost her ball, and she was having difficulty retrieving it. As I was watching this scene, I heard a voice in me, "Please help her." But I responded to that voice, "Well, it's not my child." The voice continued, "Go get the ball." I answered back, "I don't want to get involved," and I kept on walking. Then I heard another voice within myself saying that I was self-centered. Meanwhile the little girl had retrieved her ball.

This voice was something I had never experienced before.

God: I guess this must have been an amazing event for you.

Lisa: Yes, I hadn't really experienced this kind of conflict in me before, regardless I had been in similar situations. In fact,

First meeting

the thought that I should do something seldom came to me. But this conflict is not easy for me to accept because I like to feel in control.

God: I do agree it is not pleasant to have a thought that tells you what to do when you already planned what you wanted to do. So, I suppose after walking in the park, like you did, it must have been quite an experience to suddenly hear another thought from your mind, asking you to do something in a completely different direction from where your body was headed.

Lisa: Yes, I usually have a direction and I focus on getting there. But now there is another obstacle. It seems like on the way I also need to fulfill some other thoughts that may come. Is that correct?

God: Yes, I think it is exactly the way you say it. You need to fulfill your everyday goals as well as the thoughts coming from your mind, or your conscience, if you want to become a lovely being. But if you choose to reject the thoughts of your conscience, I guess you will just be what you call a normal person.

Lisa: So, in other words, You want to say if I am a person who only pursues my everyday needs in life, You will consider me to be just a 'normal' person?

God: Exactly! This kind of pursuit will only help you to survive physically intact until the last day of your life. But there is another dimension of life that you are unaware of, yet still needs to be fulfilled.

To fulfill that dimension, you have to welcome your

conscience, whose purpose is to tell you things so you can become a person who can fit to the life that is unseen by you but so real for Me.

Lisa: If I live according to Your notion, I think I will not live very comfortably here on this Earth. I will have no more freedom, because I will need to follow not only the thoughts of my physical demands, but the thoughts of my conscience as well, which according to You, prepare me for what is unseen.

I have always thought that freedom means we can fulfill whatever we want without someone or something stopping us from doing so.

God: I like your explanation of freedom, because if you use the same theory regarding your conscience, you will realize if nothing stops you from fulfilling what your conscience asks, you are free.

Lisa: That is a clever answer. But how can I fulfill what my conscience asks when my life is so full already? I wake up early to go to work and then take some classes until quite late at night. When I arrive home, I check my messages, have a snack, browse the internet, and then I organize my things for the next day.

If I may tell You, here we need to work many days and a lot of hours to make money to have what we want to have.

God: Yes, indeed, it looks like in your life you don't have so much time for anything besides working and studying.

But regardless of your activities, if you do not think about Me or if you do not satisfy your conscience, you will not feel well from now on, due to your discovery of another dimension of your being. Because this aspect was unknown to you before,

First meeting

you didn't have this conflict.

Lisa: So, it seems I am condemned to experience conflict every time I don't follow my conscience?

God: I think it is the same as when your boss asks you to do something and you do not accomplish it. Then, as you know, a conflict will come. And, therefore, you choose to obey your boss, don't you?

Lisa: Yes, of course, I'm always trying to fulfill what my boss wants.

God: But what does this boss give to you that makes you so obedient to your job, besides money or perhaps a few compliments? Nothing, regardless you are so happy to receive and to use the money your boss offers you.

Lisa: Listening to Your comments, it seems this compensation for my efforts from my boss is not a big deal for You. But for me it has been a big achievement.

God: The reason I use the example of your boss is to explain to you that if you follow your conscience, there is also something you can receive. In this case, what you can receive is peace and happiness, not just for a few seconds, but for many days. And eventually, if you are a champion to obey or to unite with your conscience, you will have the opportunity to meet My presence from today and for eternity.

Lisa: I think that You are offering me a very good deal concerning my eternal life. But still, what seems of major concern to me right now is that I have a job, a good place to live, friends, and some time for relaxing on my weekends.

God: I believe you talk about the most important aspects of your life. But what you do not know is that your physical existence on this planet is so minuscule compared to the life you are going to live afterwards. It is extremely difficult to comprehend why people as intelligent as you do not take the concept of the real life more seriously.

Lisa: Here we do not have a lot of education about the life that You consider to be so important. Instead, when we are young, our parents tell us that we need to study to get a good job, as if our job is the only purpose in our life. We believe our parents as well as our society, who both seem to have the same concern that everyone should strive to get a good job.

God: From where I am I can see every human being moving from place to place similar to the ants or the bees. Ants move very fast in an organized way. They have a good system for living in a community and they keep a certain political order. It seems you copied your idea of the meaning of your physical existence from them, didn't you?

Lisa: I don't know where we got the inspiration to create our existence the way it is. But one thing is for sure, if we do not have money we look poor and miserable. For this reason we conclude we need to have a job and to work hard. This way we can at least live in a pleasant environment.

God: If I had thought that human beings should be similar to ants, I think I would have created them differently. First of all, I would not have permitted humans to live for so many years, which gives them the time necessary to distinguish themselves

First meeting

from other creatures. Secondly, I would not have given them the desire to have relationships with fellow humans. And, of course, they would never be able to imagine that I exist, nor need to have a conscience or a heart, since they would be destined to just return to dust.

Lisa: I never thought much about all these things You talk about. But I do feel a sense of wanting to live with my heart and according to my conscience, and I want my life to be something more profound. I also need to say to You that I feel some pleasure in how I have been living.

God: I created a conscience inside each human being so they could receive words of wisdom to help them pave the road leading to their destiny. If they obey those words of wisdom with faith, they will find Me closer to them than they ever experienced before.

Lisa: Of course I've heard about the conscience before, but its definition was vague and usually connected to some big issue like a political or a human rights issue. Yet the way You present the conscience, it is something very personal.

God: Yes, I remember the first time I mentioned to someone on this Earth about his conscience. It was connected to an issue regarding killing another human being.
   This particular person felt that he had a right to kill, which in his time was permitted for someone in his position. Over a process of months I said to him many times, through his conscience, that it was not good to kill. When he wanted to do so his conscience reminded him, "You should not kill" and gave him a hard time. I instructed him to not disobey those words, otherwise he would regret it for many long years.

But this person did not want to believe what I said and he killed someone, and later on he struggled so much, as I had predicted. Through that situation he started to accept the importance of the conscience inside of him.

This is why this person from a long time ago testified about his experience and brought the law that you should not kill another human being.

Lisa: By listening to You I feel You have a lot of difficulty to make us understand things.

God: I do not have difficulty explaining to human beings how I created them, but the problem is that there is an element in them that wants to reject what already exists inside of them. Because of that nature, which denies everything else besides what is physical, what they can see and touch, it is difficult for Me to explain to them in detail how they are really made.

Lisa: When I listen to You, I can perceive that the idea of wanting to fulfill our daily physical desires seems to hinder us from recognizing and following what is deep inside of ourselves, like our heart or our conscience.

God: If human beings had a more peaceful nature overall and to some degree would monitor their secular ambitions, it would be easier for them to perceive there is another part within them waiting to be developed and explored, like their heart's dream.

Lisa: I don't fully understand what You mean when You talk about having a more peaceful nature. I believe that with a more assertive nature we can accomplish many things, and with the desire to advance we can surmount many obstacles.

First meeting

Without a certain amount of aggressiveness I would never have achieved as much as I have.

God: When you observe animals, you will realize the chief of the pack or the chief of the family is the one who shows a lot of aggressiveness towards others. I think an animal can be proud to demonstrate this kind of superiority. But some part of you sees this behavior as being pretty barbaric, belonging only to a system of survival. I created it like that to make sure a species can maintain its natural strength and beauty. Through that process disease, deformations and other possible degenerations disappear and keep that species qualified to survive.

If I created humans to function according to the same law, it would be understandable why they are so aggressive. However, I did not create you or other human beings according to that law.

Lisa: Do You know, many religious people say that You created us in Your image? That is perhaps why we have a tendency, myself included, to believe that the way we are is what You created us to be. I feel there is nothing wrong with pursuing my dream, regardless I sometimes need to climb over somebody who seems to be less qualified.

God: If I created human beings that way, I think I made a big mistake and that eventually there will be no more human beings left on your Earth. This is because the aggressive nature that exists inside of you could destroy not just a few human beings for the sake of your own survival, but could destroy all human beings. You seem to have an aggressive nature that is worse than what any animal has ever done for its survival.

Lisa: So, You want to say that You are not responsible for our nature that acts so aggressively against our fellow human beings?

God: My original idea was to create human beings in My image. I intended them to be capable of loving like I love and of relating with other human beings through their hearts. Originally I planned for human beings to be able to communicate with Me as well.

This is the reason I created an organ called the conscience, so you can be guided to build a nature of goodness equal to what I am. I created humans with a mind so they can be capable of creating things like I can create, and also, to have the capacity to sense how to relate harmoniously with their fellow humans.

Lisa: Then why don't we resemble Your idea, which sounds very fine to me?

God: Well, I am happy My idea looks good to you because so far this idea has been neglected by human beings in general, as well as by you. This idea is My original plan that is inside all human beings. Yet, it is this plan that is so difficult for human beings to believe in.

Lisa: If it is inside of us, why do we have such difficulty to believe in it?

God: Let me explain a little bit about your history. There was a time, not too long ago, when human beings did not have as much knowledge or sensitivity as the people living in your day.

At that time, most people valued only human bodily strength, to the point anybody who was weaker didn't feel

First meeting

safe to walk outside his or her home without being attacked. As well, anyone who had the tendency to think or to use his head in some way was ridiculed or even killed. Therefore the question I have for you, Lisa, is why did humans beings have such a destructive nature toward something that today seems to be so important and appreciated, such as the ability to gain knowledge or the right to feel safe when walking on the streets?

Lisa: Yes, I remember being shocked when I learned about how people with new ideas were treated throughout history. I couldn't comprehend why it was such a major problem for people to accept that human beings could bring new ideas or have their own opinions.

God: Throughout the history of human beings everything that was more invisible than their hands and feet was difficult for them to believe in. Therefore, when someone discovered a new theory, a major struggle would occur around it. This is one of the foremost reasons why history is so full of violence, suffering and destruction.

Lisa: If I dare ask a question, God, may I ask if You were there during all those miserable times in human history?

God: Well, it is not so easy for Me to just say yes or no.
Surely, I was in the midst of these struggles because I was the one who initiated the discoveries of the invisible side of human beings. However, someone else was trying to push away and demolish everything that was not visible for the sake of making human beings believe they are just matter alone.
To explain it in a different way, when I had an opportunity to influence human beings, I sought to pass through the human

heart and conscience. Because of the experiences produced by My efforts, people started to create many new philosophies. This is the reason religious thought or an awareness of the spiritual dimension started to increase.

But then, when I was no longer allowed to be there, the one who controls the flesh of human beings was directing them to wipe out every trace of knowledge connected to what is invisible, or connected to Me.

Lisa: I'm writing everything You say and somehow I'm overwhelmed by what I'm writing. because I realize I don't have any idea of who You are or what You have been through.

I feel a need to concentrate and I perceive my pen writing at such a high speed on the paper. I'm surprised that my hand doesn't cramp, because, You know, in our time we don't write by hand so much. Therefore I guess something is helping me.

God: If I say to you it is Me who is helping you it is not exact. It is actually the energy you feel in this moment that allows you to write so fast and without pain in your hand. Would you agree that you feel something, or do you consider our meeting is occuring on a purely intellectual level?

Lisa: I am not sure what to tell You, but yes, maybe I can write so easily because there is a feeling that comes along with Your words.

God: I think, Lisa, after this conversation, which I hope was instructive for you, I will now remove Myself. Then you can continue to fulfill your physical dream, which I still feel a bit uncomfortable to interrupt. Maybe if you make room in the midst of your daily activities, I will try again to pass through the channel you give to Me.

First meeting

Lisa's comments to the reader

After this event, amazed at what had happened to me, I continued to write down whatever I could recall from my conversation with God, for my own sake as well as for anyone else that might read about this someday. While talking with God I had lost sense of time and place, but when I was alone again I realized about an hour had passed. I was so surprised at how much could happen in my mind and how many emotions could pass through me during that period of time.

What took place overwhelmed me, but another part of me was already wishing God would come again, and that I would be more ready to receive what He would tell me.

SECOND MEETING

Second meeting

It was a lovely spring day and I was so happy to be able to go to the park in the afternoon. It was amazing to see all the flowers, plants, and new leaves, with their different shapes and colors. Birds were singing and the buds on a large magnolia tree had burst into full bloom. There were children playing ball and lots of people strolling about. Everything put me in a good mood.

Then in the evening, in the midst of getting prepared for the next day, I thought I heard my name. Knowing I was alone, I was quite startled. I looked around, turning my head from left to right, concerned that there might be someone in my home, but there was silence. Soon my worry disappeared and my focus returned to what I was doing.

Then I heard my name again. This time it was more distinct and clear, and I asked who was there. The voice responded to me, "I am the One who spoke to you last time."

God: I would like to approach you so I can speak to you. Would you desire that, or shall I come at another time, yet unknown to Me?

Lisa: Oh, I'm so happy that You can come back again after so many weeks! Last time I learned a lot from Your explanations, and I found that they had the power to transform my viewpoint about several things.

God: The reason I could come to you this time is because you were very grateful today. I guess you went somewhere. You had an attitude of recognizing everything you saw. This is what permitted Me to approach you. The moment you said My name, when you saw the flowers of all different colors, I felt I could come and talk with you.

Lisa: Oh yes, I remember that event. It was when I was in the park admiring all the hyacinths and daffodils that looked so colorful and smelled so good. At that moment I felt obliged to call Your name. Actually, I didn't really consciously call Your name, I just said, "Oh my God, how beautiful it is," and then I started thinking about our last meeting.

God: For Me to approach human beings they need to be in a certain state and have a specific kind of thought. First, they need to be peaceful or calm, or something similar to that. Next, they need to be grateful about something. Finally, they need to call My name, or have some kind of thought about Me. If people can maintain these three aspects for a certain period of time, then I can approach them. This period of time needs to be not just for a few seconds but for several minutes or longer.

Lisa: So, I guess I did that but I was not really aware of what I was doing. It seems like it happened by accident, or something like that.

God: Well, it is indeed a problem to not be aware of what you are doing. That is the reason many of you call this event when I come close to you, a miracle, and why this event can take place so seldom.

But normally, nothing happens by accident, and if something appears accidental, it is only because human beings do not understand how to use the mechanisms of their mind to achieve certain states, for example the dimension of peace. But if they were to learn about these mechanisms, it would

Second meeting

be similar to learning about anything else they have already discovered.

Lisa: So what You are saying is, if I want Your presence close to me, I need to be peaceful and grateful, and at the same time think about You or call Your name. Is this correct?

God: Theoretically that is correct. If you achieve the junction of these elements, being absolutely grateful and calm for a certain time period and thinking about Me, then I can approach you.

But there is another reality that can prevent that connection. If you want Me to approach you in a particular manner, or with a specific expectation, that will destroy the base needed for Me to perceive you.

Lisa: You want to say if I expect You to come in a certain way, this can stop You from coming?

God: Many people call My name quite often and they also know how to become peaceful to some extent. But they have another obstacle, which they are possibly not aware of. If a person has a specific thought regarding how I should act towards him or her, that thought can destroy the connection.

To give an example, if a person wishes I would repeat the same thought I perhaps had already given him or her at another meeting, that wish could be an obstacle for My approach.

Lisa: It looks like it's really difficult for You to come to us, whether it's someone like me, who doesn't think about You often, or someone who deliberately tries to pursue You. It seems neither one of us has a guarantee of meeting You again.

Is this correct?

God: Personally, I suffer immensely because of this reality. I begin to relate with someone and at first it looks easy. But soon that person, maybe even you in the near future, has the concept that he automatically knows Me. Or, maybe you will have the feeling, as many people have, that you are special because I have approached you.

Believing you know Me because I tell you something is an immense obstacle for Me to continue relating with you. But even worse is to choose to believe you are special because I talk to you. This thought would make Me turn My back on you, if I had a back. And, until you abandoned that view of yourself and recreated a base of innocence, I would again be unknown to you.

Lisa: I have had a chance to meet people who told me with conviction that they believed in You or knew You. After some time, I discovered that I started to feel uncomfortable with them, to the point I wanted to avoid them, especially when they repeated their thoughts about You. However, I never imagined You would also dislike this situation.

God: What I reject about this situation is that people often change their character when they start to believe they know something about Me. And usually, the character they develop is the opposite of who I am. Because of that, I can no longer approach them regardless of what I said to them before or what they learned from Me.

Lisa: So, if I create some expectation towards You, You will not be able to come, even though I learn to call Your name, is this correct?

Second meeting

God: Yes. Many people were taught they should call My name and then I would be there, instantly.

But if you check how many of these people who call My name are actually able to perceive My presence, the number is infinitely small. This is because they forget to create a certain attitude of calmness, gratitude and humility within themselves, which are the perfect attributes for Me to be able to approach them over and over.

Lisa: I have heard that the Buddhist religion teaches how to find a stage of peace. In light of what You have been telling me, maybe I should choose their way in order to meet You.

God: I will say that the idea to find peace within oneself should be a fundamental goal of human beings. But this goal cannot be achieved if people do not also want to meet Me as part of their goal. The wish to find nirvana cannot be achieved by will, by tradition, or by desire alone, but only if I am invited in the midst of it.

Therefore I will say to you, be grateful about what you see and connect this gratefulness to Me. This is the essence to find peace within yourself and the prerequisite for you to meet Me or for Me to meet you.

If among human beings there is some knowledge that promotes a state of peacefulness and gratefulness, you can learn from it, but you must also learn to welcome Me in the midst of it.

Lisa: I think that becoming more peaceful sounds like a good idea, but is not so easy to achieve. You see, human beings have the capacity to keep many thoughts in our minds and we also value that ability highly. The more we can think, the more we have the tendency to say to ourselves that we are smart.

But I wonder if these multitude of thoughts, coming from

who knows where, can co-exist with Your concept of calmness and serenity? Can we be thinkers and still achieve serenity, a state that seems not to have any thoughts?

God: If you have studied about the different philosophies of your people, you would realize that philosophers have the power to influence what people consider to be right or wrong. For example, if many people choose what a certain philosopher considers to be right, and neglect to value something else because this philosopher considers it to be wrong, a movement is created that automatically produces an affirmation of what that philosopher promotes. In other words, we can say that a philosopher creates a certain sense of value and other people of that time will tend to want to choose that value as the way of pursuing their happiness.

The reason I say this to you is to explain that there have been different values according to different time periods. Usually people only follow what is considered as highly valued in their time. For example, if thinking is considered to be of high value, then not thinking is seen to be of low value and therefore the people of that time period will learn to think.

But at a different time and place of human history, when learning to be peaceful and emptying the mind of too many thoughts, like what the Buddhists strive to achieve, was considered to be of a high value, many human beings chose this value as their life goal.

Lisa: Does this mean that whatever I think of as valuable is actually based on some philosopher who gave his thought to the people around him and eventually influenced the whole society? Is my sense of right and wrong based upon the thoughts of a particular person who just decided, as You said, what was right and what was wrong?

Second meeting

God: What I want to tell you is not really about right or wrong, but about helping you to put yourself in a place where I can come to you. That place is similar to a junction, a meeting place, like an address that you give to a friend when you want to meet him or her.

Lisa: It seems to me You don't like it so much when we uphold a specific value or belief. But I feel that we need to value certain things, because if we value nothing, then life would have no meaning.

God: It looks like you are panicking a little bit based on what I tell you. I will give you an example, hoping that what I say can be more understandable to you.

If you go to a garage and you observe a mechanic, you will realize that he takes out each piece of an engine, cleans each piece regardless of its size, and then places each one aside in a specific location, remembering very well where each one was initially. Then he puts them all back into their correct positions.

What is interesting about this person is that he does not consider any piece as being right or another as being wrong, regardless of its size or function. In spite of each piece's weak or strong points, he recognizes each one as having immense value.

It is amazing to see how he cares for each piece because he perceives that each one has the same value in relationship to what he wants to build. In doing so he displays a similar nature as I have, even though he might not know it. Surely, I can recognize My character in him.

But the reason you demonstrate confusion is because you want to choose one aspect of human nature over another aspect. And that is not acceptable.

Lisa: Indeed, as I follow what You want to tell me, I can only agree with Your example of a mechanic who knows a screw has the same value as a hose or a pump and so forth. But fixing an engine so that it can function properly is a physical example, and I am not sure if this can be applied to something more abstract, like ideas.

God: Today, as well as many years ago, a philosopher was believed to be a philosopher because he had a tendency to choose one thought over another one. In other words, his strength always came from choosing a specific category of thought and at the same time rejecting another category of thought. Because of this situation, the direction of every nation went from left to right and then again from right to left, resembling a person who cannot walk a straight line, or a person who is intoxicated.

So if, in the past, people felt being calm and serene was the best philosophy of the time, they chose that as their value and rejected any person who believed another way. Likewise if today the mood is to think and to value thinking, I believe the people of this time will reject any philosophy that promotes peacefulness or serenity.

Thus, I think My example of the mechanic fits very well to the world of thought.

Lisa: I am writing down everything You say. It is quite long but I understand Your point now. To make sure, did You want to say that we should value each aspect of our being instead of choosing one aspect over another one?

God: Yes, I think you perceive My point now. I felt before you were a little bit nervous, but I could also see you were trying to control yourself to allow Me to give you My view, which I

Second meeting

appreciate, because usually this is exactly My difficulty with human beings.

Lisa: Yes, it's not so easy to listen to what You have to say. Like You said, we don't just have thoughts, but our thoughts are connected to our values, and this makes us defensive at times—especially, like just now, if what You say is quite different from what I had already learned.

God: The difficulty of changing someone's viewpoint, whether it be it today or sometime in the past, is not that you and the people of the Earth have a wrong point of view, but when you choose something as being right, you have a strong tendency to demolish the value of something else that, in another time, people chose as being right.

If you therefore believe that today you are more civilized or educated than people in the past, I will say no. What is true is that you choose a distinct thought that is different from your parents' or grandparents' thought, for example. But usually this achievement makes you believe you are better educated, or right, compared to someone from the past. And that makes you become wrong.

Lisa: From this conversation, I realize that actually every idea people have can be good or useful, and I should never reject a thought that doesn't seem to fit with what I think I already know. When I recall what You tried to tell me about the mechanic who valued every piece of an engine, I can now understand why You appreciate that kind of person.

God: So, to repeat, in order for you to meet Me, you must first value every aspect of what I tell you. If you only choose a specific thought and value this thought as being the highest one, you may reject what I tell you the next time, which will make it impossible for us to meet each other again.

When people begin to only value thinking many thoughts as being right, and neglect to realize that being calm and serene is also important, it is normal that their minds start to spin with so many thoughts, to the point they cannot stop.

Lisa: It is true, I appreciate being able to think, especially when I am at work or trying to make a conversation with someone. But it is also true, when I am in my home and have the desire to stop thinking in order to relax, I often find myself incapable of doing that. Many times it comes to a point where I say to myself, privately, that I will go crazy.

God: I believe what you say is correct and that right now you are being sincere with Me by accepting to reveal what happens to you when you are in your home. I can also see, when you are at your job, that the ability to think allows you to carry out the particular job you have.

Lisa: Personally I am very proud of being able to analyze things when I need to make a workplan or give a report or communicate with my colleagues. But now, because You came to me and initiated a new wish in me—the wish to relate with You—I realize I need to expand my viewpoint and not overvalue this aspect of thinking.

God: Value is an interesting thing. In your world, value is often recognized through money. When people want something very much and it is hard to attain, then the cost or the value of that object can go up and up. But if it becomes more easily available, then the value changes direction and goes down, like passing over a peak.

Second meeting

Sometimes, when an item is extremely rare or even one-of-a-kind, the value can rise to a level hard to comprehend. I have heard your museums contain things like this: you call them 'priceless'. Honestly speaking, I do not comprehend that rule so well, do you?

Lisa: We put a monetary value on things for the purpose of allowing people to buy them. Many times, the higher the value we attach to something, the more people want to have it, making the price go even higher. Then another producer might take that object and produce it in greater quantities, causing the price to decrease. As well, a new fad might come along, and therefore the previous fad just fades away. Does this make sense to You?

God: Right now I am listening to what you are saying and I guess I also start to understand. It seems that, based on the circumstances surrounding an object, its value changes. Even though the value in terms of an object's usefulness can stay the same, the price can change a lot within a short time. I think now I can comprehend why the people of your civilization tend to more easily value a baby or a child, which is something new, and disvalue an old person, something aged and used. I believe it must be similar to what you have just explained to Me.

Lisa: Well, honestly speaking, I'm surprised how You put everything together so fast. I had never come to that conclusion. But it is possible, as You say, that we value more highly what is new than what is old or out of fashion.

God: I hope you understand My point today, to value what you newly discover without removing the value of what you already know, and without considering it is out of fashion, as you say. So, if you value thinking, I will say it is wonderful. But if you now value becoming serene, I will also say it is wonderful. And, if you accept to value calling Me in the midst of your life, I will say that is wonderful as well. Therefore each thing has the same value regardless each event is different.

If all the parts of yourself were the same, you would not be able to function. Therefore, it is good you have different parts within you and that they function differently. What is missing in your concept is to value every part of yourself equally.

If you look at each member or organ of your body as having the same value, you can begin to use every part well. But if you choose to value only a specific function, elevating its value and decreasing the value of other functions, then you can only find chaos and frustration in your body, because some part will be neglected, to the point it can decide to go on strike or to make itself sick, or even allow itself to die.

Lisa: What You recommend to me is to begin appreciating every aspect of my body and my mind, and to value both the new and the old.

God: Yes, Lisa. If you train yourself to value one flower evenly with another flower or one person evenly with another person, regardless of their differences, you will begin to appreciate many things in your life. At the same time it will be much easier for you to be grateful and peaceful, which as I said before is the necessary attitude to meet Me.

Lisa: Well, I can see that to be able to meet You requires something from my part. I cannot guarantee You that in the future I will be able to be in the right place.

Still, I am so grateful that You could come to me today and give Your thoughts, and I want to say thank you for everything.

Second meeting

Lisa's comments to the reader

At the end of our conversation I was beginning to feel very tired. I think I felt that way because the dialogue was profound and I was not so familiar with the ideas. Then to be polite, I just said thank you, and God left.

Therefore, I realized how easy it is to end a dialogue with God, especially if I compare that situation with meeting with my colleagues or friends. They don't disappear when I make certain gestures that show I am a bit tired. But when we communicate with God, it seems any outside thought or desire can disturb the dialogue.

So, if in case you are also in a position where you can hear God, I want to suggest to you to stay calm as long as you can and not to think about getting up for a snack or going to the bathroom. If you divert your attention, I don't think you will find God again in that moment.

Right after this conversation, I became aware that I was still in my room and God was not. I felt like there was a hole inside of me, a feeling I never imagined to have.

Later I wrote in my diary, trying to be as sincere as possible about this experience, since I felt He would be happy if I was sincere. Then I closed my diary, hoping to write in it another day, if God could come to visit me again.

THIRD MEETING

Third meeting

On one particular day I longed so much to meet God. It had been a few weeks since He had spoken with me. All this time I tried to remember His words, to be grateful and to call His name, especially on this day, as I hoped He would be able to come to see me again. I cleaned my house all morning, eager to satisfy Him. It felt good to do so, regardless it is so easy to mess it up again, even when living alone.

Honestly, I felt a little bit nervous when I imagined Him coming. On the other hand, I felt quite eager. A few times during the day I prepared my paper, just in case He might come and speak. The last time it was difficult to write everything down, and afterwards, it was hard to remember all that was said. After all, everything is in my mind—what He speaks, and how I respond.

Yes, today felt so special, because I was anticipating meeting Someone extremely important. I was surprised to see myself so excited, when I am usually so cool.

Since the morning I had been hoping God would come, but I hadn't heard anything all day, just my heart beating faster from time to time. I kept hope until the evening time. A few times I went to the window of my apartment, watching the light start to fade, until it became quite dark. Different thoughts came to me and I started to believe that the possibility that He would come was over for that day.

I decided to prepare myself to go to bed and I took a shower. Then, just when I was finished, I heard a deep voice calling my name, asking me if I was there. Shaking I answered, "Yes I am here." Then God asked me, "Were you waiting for Me today?" But maybe because I was too shy or just afraid to say the truth, I said, "Oh yes, I was thinking about You just a few minutes ago."

The Rebirth of God and Lisa

God: Do you remember what I told you last time, which for you was quite some time ago, regardless for Me it seems like it was just yesterday?

Lisa: Yes, I remember Your lesson, because I read over my notes several times and thought about what You said.

God: So, it looks like you tried to educate yourself based on what I spoke about.

Lisa: Yes, I tried to remind myself of what You told me. I especially remember You said that I should value everything around me equally. You also said I need to recognize that I have a conscience.

God: Well, that is very good. So I believe everything is going well for you now?

Lisa: Well, I must admit, living here on Earth with so many daily activities, it seems easy to forget what You taught me. Maybe it's because I don't always see where I can use Your words. You see, each day has its routine—I wake up, go to work and do many other things along the way. The thoughts You give me don't appear to be so necessary in order to get me through each day.

God: So, seen from the perspective of your life as you just now explained it to Me, does this mean what I recommend to you to adopt in your life is not important, and because you don't feel the need and the pressure to fulfill it, you should abandon what I say?

Lisa: No, not exactly. I just wanted to explain to You why it

Third meeting

is so easy to for me to forget Your words.

God: Then, if I take your situation seriously, should I stop trying to find human beings who can learn from what I have to say, because they are so busy or because their life is not connected to the life I ask them to be concerned about?

Lisa: In some ways I would say yes, but I feel it's rude to tell You that. Also, if I think that way, it means I believe I am not capable of learning anything from You, and therefore am destined to always stay the same. But I don't want this to happen because I have a hard time to like myself the way I am.

God: Then, should I continue to look for someone or should I stop looking, because human beings are more concerned about where they put their feet than about what they will become?

Lisa: I think You should continue to try to give Your thoughts, even though I myself have encountered the difficulty of including them in the midst of my daily life. Yet, theoretically at least, it seems good to have an awareness of what You have revealed to me, such as the idea that I have a conscience and I need to obey it, or that I need to accept every part of myself as equally valuable.

God: So, you realize that from the moment I met you and introduced various thoughts, many complex events you had never experienced before started to take place within you? Before I spoke with you, you never thought much about anything deeper than the desires of your secular ambitions, which, I guess, were fulfilled through your daily activities, in particular through your job.

The Rebirth of God and Lisa

Lisa: Yes. For example, I discovered that from the time You first spoke to me I became aware of my conscience asking me different things, simple things like to be gentler when I talk to someone or to call someone when I know they are lonely. I also realize that if I don't follow my conscience, then I feel some kind of guilt.

God: What do you mean by saying you feel some kind of guilt? The word 'guilt' does not exist here. What exists is, did you achieve it, or did you not achieve it.

Lisa: Well, all I know is that if I cannot accomplish my desires, especially the demands coming from my conscience, I feel bad.

God: So, every time you want to achieve something and you cannot, for whatever reason, you are going to feel bad? Indeed, if this is the case, I think it is better to never want to do anything, or to never hear your conscience, because you can already predict you will feel guilty afterwards.

The word 'guilty' is an extremely strong word, don't you think, and not so pleasant for you to hear, especially if it is connected to you. Isn't it usually used for someone who breaks the law in your world, for example, for a criminal?

Does this now mean that everything you wish to do becomes a law, to the point that if you cannot accomplish it, you are condemned to be guilty like a criminal? Is this what is going on inside of you?

Lisa: Well, yes, it feels something like that. One thing is for sure, from the day You started speaking to me I have more feelings of guilt than I ever had before. And these feelings are sometimes quite unpleasant, to the point I started to believe

Third meeting

that if I stopped listening to my conscience for a short time, I would feel better.

God: Did that work?

Lisa: Yes, to some degree I could feel free like I used to, and fulfill my wishes without thinking much about whether they were right or wrong.

But I had already begun to enjoy some of the changes I experienced within myself when I followed my conscience, and I didn't like the idea of reverting to the person I used to be.

It's just that the guilty feeling bothered me when I couldn't fulfill what my conscience asked me.

God: I think I understand now what you mean by the word 'guilt'. Therefore should we agree, when someone does not follow what he knows to be a law, he will feel guilty? This means, regardless how minuscule the request from your conscience, or a request from another person, who is actually in the same position as your conscience, if you do not achieve it, it is understandable that since you broke the law, you will feel guilty.

Maybe you don't know it, but the law that makes you feel most guilty if you disobey it is the law connected to relationships, in other words, the law that maintains peace between human beings. But, if you can find a law that is not connected to a relationship with someone else, and if you break that law, you will be surprised that you feel less guilty about it.

Lisa: Well, I never thought about it that way. Your answer is very interesting.

God: Thank you for your compliment.

To continue My point, if you hear inside of yourself to clean the house for your own self and you do not fulfill it, then you might feel disappointed or tell yourself that you are not organized, or give some other explanation for your behavior, but you will not feel guilty.

Yet, if you decide to clean the house for the sake of your roommate or your friend and you do not fulfill that idea, then you will be shocked to see that a feeling of guilt will be born inside of you. Do you see My point?

Lisa: I hear very well what You're saying, but I'm not sure what to think about it right now. One thing is for sure, Your view is quite new for me.

God: Can I continue?

Lisa: Yes, please do.

God: What is also interesting about guilt is the more you value what you want to do and you don't achieve it, the more the feeling of guilt will amplify.

For example, if you like someone very, very much and you say to him that you will meet him in a particular restaurant at 8:00 p.m. but then you cannot arrive on time, you will feel very guilty. On the other hand, if you do not care if you make it or not to a meeting, in other words, you don't value the meeting with that person, if you do not arrive on time you will easily find many excuses for your lateness. And, the most interesting thing is that you will not feel guilty at all.

Lisa: So, this means, if I choose to care about relating with You and I cannot fulfill what You ask me, I will feel greater guilt?

Third meeting

God: The guilt is heavy if you highly care about or value the order you receive, as well as the one giving the order, but you don't obey. However, if you decide to obey, that mass of guilt can be transformed into a mass of pleasure. This process works like a system of balances.

For example, if you put vegetables on one side of the balance and on the other side you put the weights, the vegetables symbolize the idea, and the weights symbolize your deeds concerning that idea. Based on the equilibrium between both of them, you will have different dimensions of feeling at the center point, which is you.

In the same way, if you have an idea that you value highly, or in other words has a lot of weight, and if you do not fulfill this idea with your actions, it will tilt the balance and provoke a negative feeling in you, like guilt, showing you are not in balance.

But I also know, according to how I see your people acting, the most common way to remove guilt is to remove the value connected to any request or any wish you can hear from inside yourself or from any person who comes close to you. Regardless of this ability to devalue things, this road will not help you become a great and valuable being.

Lisa: So, it looks like removing the value from my wish might remove my guilt but will hurt my growth.

God: That is correct. As well, if your wish has nothing to do with helping or pleasing someone else besides yourself, you will not feel guilty because that wish has no value concerning expanding and improving the condition of your inner being. Only when you start to want to please someone, in that moment will you expand your value. If you don't achieve that expansion of your value, you will stay empty, and that emptiness will make you perceive guilt.

 *The Rebirth of God and Lisa*

Lisa: So, if I seldom felt guilty before, is it because I never wanted to please anyone but myself?

God: Correct.

Lisa: The truth is, I have lived for many years trying to please myself. Much of that time I felt content, until something changed and I started to experience loneliness. In the midst of that loneliness I continued to try to please myself, trying to get back my old feelings. Even though I sometimes did feel better, very soon I found loneliness returning.
   I couldn't understand why this was happening to me. Then one day You came to visit me.

God: Well, did you feel guilty after I came to see you or did you feel good that I came?

Lisa: I felt good. Actually, I was very pleased that You came.

God: The reason you did not feel guilty when I came to visit you was because you accepted the idea of My coming to you. But let's imagine you refused to welcome or to listen to Me, when deep inside your heart you were looking for Me. Do you believe you would feel peaceful and happy, or would you feel guilty after that?

Lisa: I think I would have felt guilty, regardless of the fact that when You came the first time, I didn't know anything about You and therefore hadn't identified the longing inside me as my heart looking for You. I certainly know if I pushed You away today, I would feel very guilty about this behavior.

God: Therefore, to not take the road of guilt anymore, you

Third meeting

need to agree with what you hear inside you, and, in general, with what happens around you. Then, instead of feeling guilty, you will feel happy and peaceful. Uniting with your conscience and with your environment will instantly give you a certain quantity of peace.

Lisa: I think I would immensely prefer the feeling of peace to the feeling of guilt.

God: I am very pleased you prefer to feel peaceful. It is important for Me that you experience joy and peace, because in that kind of state I can come to see you.

Lisa: So far, I haven't focused much on making myself peaceful or happy. I've just tried to call Your name from time to time, hoping You could come.

God: Is that so?

Lisa: To be honest with You, many times I felt the wish to meet You, and I tried to call You, hoping You would come like today.

God: Oh, really?

Lisa: Well, I realize that when You visit me, some change occurs in me. Last time You came, Your way of thinking affected me so deeply that sometimes it made me feel uncomfortable. This was the reason that for awhile, I tried to forget about You. Then, after a few weeks passed, I started to long for You again, and began to call Your name again.

God: Do you feel guilty if you call Me and I don't come?

51

   *The Rebirth of God and Lisa*

Lisa: No. I feel some kind of sadness or longing, though.

God: But if you forget to call Me when you know that you should call Me, do you then feel guilty?

Lisa: A few times I told myself that I wanted to remember to think about You and because I couldn't do it, I did feel some guilt. Not knowing how to deal with that guilt, I started to reject the whole idea of calling You and instead asked, "Why doesn't God respond to me when I want Him to respond?"

God: To help you understand what you just told Me, I will explain to you again how, instead of guilt, you can feel peace and happiness. If you cannot remember to think of Me in order to permit Me to come, then instead of getting upset, you just need to admit that you forgot to call Me and try again. When you try again, it means you once more unite with your wish to call Me, and therefore peace will come inside of you.

Lisa: It just seems that guilt automatically comes when I don't fulfill something.

God: Looking from a technical point of view I will say yes. As I explained before, if you make a plan to please someone and you break that plan, guilt comes as a result. But the law works the same way on the other side. When you fulfill your plan, then another feeling emerges, the feeling of happiness.

Lisa: It looks like the road to feeling happy is fragile. At any moment, when we don't fulfill what we hear from our conscience, guilt can appear and happiness can disappear.

God: When I listen to your response, indeed it seems for

Third meeting

people like you that the road to feeling good is truly fragile.

But I think it doesn't have to be that way. If you highly value someone and if you desire to have a relationship of peace and happiness with that someone, wouldn't you want to follow the advice of your conscience, in order to always be at peace with yourself and with the one you value? Or would you prefer to disobey your conscience, so you would always be a guilty being in front of the one you want to value highly?

Lisa: Rationally, it doesn't make sense to not want to unite with what creates peace and joy inside of me. But I think it's not easy to discover the causes of our emotions.

However, the way You explain things to me is quite clear. Everything seems to have a certain logic, and everything I do or I don't do is connected to a feeling. You have also explained about the laws of relationship, which I really appreciate.

God: I will give you My view about how things exist around you. Let us take the weather for instance. When you observe the weather, what you are concerned about is whether it is raining or sunny, or whether it is cold or hot. These aspects of the weather can seem capricious, but there is a technical aspect to them. A particular weather is caused by low or high pressure, and the balance between the two ensures an overall good climate.

In a similar way, if you want to have a good moment, you must follow a certain law. Your thoughts, representing low pressure, and your actions, representing high pressure, are both the cause of your feelings, or in other words, your weather. If you do not balance them, you will have limited good weather. However, if you follow your good thoughts with good actions, you will have many good moments.

The Rebirth of God and Lisa

Lisa: Well, your example really helps me to see where my feelings come from, like joy or guilt. I admit I need to become more aware of that.

God: So, because now you know how to create joy and peace, will you prefer to agree with your conscience and try to achieve what it asks you, in spite of the short moments of difficulty required to do so? Conversely, the more you choose to disagree with and disobey your conscience, the more you will create a different emotion, that of guilt, which is very cold.

I would like to make another point. If you deny all the wishes of your conscience or the requests of others, then what is left is only how to fulfill your own wishes in order to bring joy to yourself. But that joy is short-lived, and you will quickly perceive loneliness again.

Lisa: I believe that even though I will experience both good moments as well as difficult moments, it will be worthwhile to drive myself in Your direction, a road so far unknown to me. Up until You came into my life, I only tried to please my own self by buying everything I wished or by looking at everything my eyes wished to see, until I was tired.

Yes, I experienced many moments of boredom and loneliness, walking from shop to shop, or from one place to another, hoping that something new or different would happen. Maybe You do not know what I am talking about, but I believe many here on Earth would understand what I am talking about, maybe too well.

I will try to go where You wish to see me go. One thing is for sure, that I wish to have joy for a longer period of time than I have experienced so far.

Thank You, my God.

God: Good-bye Lisa, for now.

Third meeting

Lisa's comments to the Reader

This meeting was different from the other two. What struck me was how smart God was. I had always believed I was intelligent, and it fascinated me that God's knowledge had such a different dimension from what I already knew. Yet in spite of that, I didn't want to tell my friends about these conversations yet, because they might call me crazy.

I have read a lot of books in my life, and most of them were interesting, but in all sincerity, I felt I wanted to read my notes from these meetings with God over and over again, as if for the first time. Therefore I put my notebook in a special place on my nightstand, where it was readily available.

After this meeting I rested well. Maybe you remember that I had planned to rest before this meeting took place.

FOURTH MEETING

Fourth meeting

Personally, I didn't consider myself to be religious according to the traditional concept. Yet after each meeting with God, I found myself yearning more deeply to meet with Him again. I hadn't expected to feel this way, but I believed it was something good.

With the desire to meet God also came the difficulty to accept that for some reason He didn't come whenever I wanted Him to be with me. Because He didn't fulfill my wish at the time I wanted Him to, I became at times upset at myself and even at Him. When that happened I tried to push to the back of my mind all my experiences regarding my conversations with Him, which wasn't usually too difficult, because my life was always so busy. But many evenings, when things became calm, the wish that He could come to visit me would re-appear, and I would feel bad that I had been upset.

Happily, God did come to visit me again, and among other things, He talked with me about my difficulty in accepting that He didn't come whenever I wished.

In these next pages I will share with you His remarks to me.

God: I have heard you Lisa, regardless you may not be aware of it. I can perceive your new dilemma and I would like to tell you something. To briefly answer your question of why I don't come when you wish, I will simply say, "I am the God of all creation and I can come of My own volition without needing you to give Me a specific permission or direction. Why should I follow what you prescribe for Me?"

 ## The Rebirth of God and Lisa

Lisa: Does this mean I should not ask You to come?

God: When you present an invitation, can you perceive that there are different ways to offer your invitation, that will affect whether the person wants to come or not?

Lisa: Yes, how an invitation is presented is very important. When I am negotiating with a client at my job, I am careful about the way I speak, because I do know that the words I choose can create different effects. But I admit, I have never really thought carefully about the way I speak to You. Have I been demanding that You come instead of just offering an invitation to You?

God: From your remark I can perceive you are a lady who has knowledge about the effect the language you use can have on the one who listens. I hope this awareness will help you to discover from which angle you can address an invitation to Me.

Lisa: Yes, My God, I can see I need to be more aware of how I speak to You. And, I want to say sorry to You.

God: So Lisa, would you like to try again?

Lisa: Yes. I would now like to ask, "If it pleases You, could I invite You to have a conversation with me tonight?"

God: That is much better, Lisa. When you look at the way everything exists around you, Lisa, what makes the beauty is because everything has its own place, and based on this place, each thing relates with one another. In the moment you discover your place in relationship to Me, then you will know

Fourth meeting

how to relate with or to address Me.

From this viewpoint, I would like to give you an example to help you understand. When you observe your internal organs, like your liver or your heart, they do not need to think about or question their positions. Your liver does not need to tell itself it is inside your body, because it is aware that it is.

This example applies exactly to you. You do not need to think about Me for Me to be with you, because you are always with Me, like your stomach is always with your body. But what you have to learn is your position, and from there, you can develop the proper relationship with Me.

Lisa: Well, it might work that way concerning the organs inside my body, but I am not so sure if I can accept that it is natural for me to have an awareness of You.

God: If you look at the creation, you will realize things exist with a constant awareness that they are bound to the laws of the universe. This is the reason they can function as harmoniously as they do. So, if human beings can learn to accept that they also belong to a certain, perhaps different, dimension of the universe, they too can begin to have the proper relationship with the universe, and with Me.

Lisa: Yes, I do see that everything in the creation works harmoniously and therefore must be following certain laws in relationship to what is living around them. But for me it is not so natural to think that You are always with me, which, as I understand it, is the view You want to present to me.

God: Mm-hmm, I hear you.

Lisa: I'm afraid that I would need to make a lot of effort to

remind myself of that reality, if it is a reality.

God: After listening to you I could make the assumption that there is some problem with the way I created all things. I did believe I created every object in this world with the ability to perceive My presence inside of them. I made an imprint inside every plant, flower, and animal, and as well, inside every human being. Therefore, it should be natural for human beings to be conscious that I am with them.

So, Lisa, what can be the reason you have so much difficulty to be aware of My presence?

Lisa: It is difficult for me to tell You, my God, but maybe I'm created in the wrong way, perhaps with something missing inside me. The fact is, I need to make tremendous effort to remind myself of You. Besides, You are invisible, and that makes it even more complicated to remember You.

God: Does this mean you are lower than the flowers and the animals? What do you think?

Lisa: I would hope that I am not below the plants and animals. Maybe I do not have the awareness that You are with me because I do not take so much time to think about You.

God: Do you think, Lisa, you need to make so much conscious effort to think about someone to realize that person is real and exists somewhere physically?

Or do you think it is more the reality of knowing that someone exists that makes you believe that person is there?

Lisa: Although I know my friend is not far away, I still feel I need to think about her consciously from time to time, and

Fourth meeting

maybe to call or to email her, or meet her for lunch sometime, because otherwise I can tend to forget she is there.

God: Is it because you cannot always feel your friend that you need to think about her in order to recognize her existence? But if your friend had a certain presence, you would be capable of feeling her, and that would be enough evidence to remind you she is there, without you needing to make a strong effort to remember her.

Lisa: Yes, that could be.

God: When you observe a blind person, you will see this person makes many movements with his hands and feet and constantly asks if there is someone or something out there, because he cannot see. The reason human beings are always asking if I exist is not because I am not there, it is because they must have lost their sense of 'sight', or don't believe in or agree with what they sense, or simply some sense organ is just frozen. This is why they cannot feel Me.

Lisa: From your example of a blind person, I realize the reason I need to think about You is because I cannot feel You. Based on that, I will say that we are blind, regardless this expression may not fit when talking about our feelings. But it is true that we cannot feel You and therefore we need to think about You, and to do that is not easy for us as well.

God: When I listen to you I perceive you might be interested in making some relationship with Me, regardless you will encounter some difficulties in achieving that.

Lisa: Yes. Looking at my life, I perceive I am a hard worker

who likes to achieve things. I enjoy having friends and doing things together. I also like to travel to new places. And, from time to time, I try to do some volunteer work. I used to believe this was all there was to life, but now I feel there is something more.

God: If I understand and hear you well, it looks like you tried many things but you still do not feel fulfilled or satisfied. Is this the reason you want to relate with Me?

Lisa: I have tried many things in order to build my confidence and experience happiness. I find I act very secure and spontaneous in front of my friends and colleagues, to the point it seems to be my character to be that way.

However, there is a different reality inside of me. I experience many unpleasant feelings that somehow get in my way. Therefore my hope is that something can change, if I can discover how to relate with You.

God: So, you dare to believe that whatever substance I am made of, this invisible substance can change something in you?

Lisa: I can only timidly answer yes, regardless I do not have a lot of experience yet. But I will still say this is my answer to You right now.

God: Do you know, Lisa, some human beings say I am omnipotent and omnipresent; in other words, if someone wants to find Me, I am everywhere and around and within every thing.

Lisa: Yes, I have heard this kind of concept, and it seemed

Fourth meeting

rather unbelievable. But now I can sense, or maybe more wish, You could be here next to me, always.

God: Lisa, do you also know there are some people who say I am just a dream or a figment of the imagination? I guess they think that way because they see that people who have some kind of concept about Me tend to dream of something better in the future, but don't look concerned about having a plan for their present lives.

Because they observe these 'religious' people, they interpret I must be the same, like a daydream in someone's mind. They think there is no possibility I can be a reality in the lives of human beings, regardless these same people forget that they walk on top of something that clearly looks very real, but which they themselves didn't create.

Lisa: When I became a teenager, I began to look down on people who believed in Your existence, like my parents, especially my mother. Eventually I rejected my mother and her belief, which was an important part of her life. But now I feel sad about that.

God: I have seen people receive accusation because they believed in Me. This accusation comes mainly because, when someone starts to believe in Me, that person becomes simpler, or less complicated, and that creates a perception that the believer is not intelligent.

On the other side, if a person doesn't adopt a belief in Me, they create a nature the opposite of simple. They create a complicated nature, which makes them feel superior, to the point they feel the need to educate or to 'wake up' a believer.

From looking at this situation for so long, I have felt so much pain.

The Rebirth of God and Lisa

Lisa: As I listen to you, I realize I was that accuser. I thought my mother was an uneducated woman. She didn't know much about what I was learning at the time and what I considered to be important. I also realize now, in accusing her I was not only against my mother but against You as well.

As I say this, I feel many things inside of me.

God: Yes, I believe you must have many feelings. And, in case you have a hard time to believe in Me, you can believe in these feelings, even though they are invisible like Me.

Lisa: You certainly know how to make a convincing point, my God.

God: So, does this mean that well-educated human beings like you, Lisa, now have the possibility to think about Me and to imagine Me being with them? At another time, when you were acquiring knowledge, you were surely working hard to exclude Me from every possible thought or idea in your life, isn't that so?

Lisa: I am so sorry for what I did to You. Today I can hear in myself the wish to have a relationship with You, even though it is not so clear how that can happen or what I should do.

But at least I can tell You, this is my wish.

God: I am happy, Lisa, that you said 'sorry'. It is true you were against Me as well as against your mother, and you even tried to discourage other people from believing in and relating with Me, in spite of the multitude of difficulties they already faced in achieving their desire.

But I will say, the fact you say 'sorry' is like using a sponge full of soap and removing what was not bright in you.

Fourth meeting

Saying sorry is the greatest action you can take when you see something dark and want to make it bright.

Lisa: Now I can, to some degree, understand what I did to my mother and also to You, by rejecting the possibility that I could relate with You. I believe a lot of people must have also done the same thing, and I feel sorry about that.

God: Thank you to be concerned about My situation. Now, I can explain to you that in order to relate with Me, the most important thing is to have a nature that to some extent resembles My brightness.

Lisa: I see.

God: There is another point of view I would like you to be aware of, in case you want to have a relationship with Me.

Many people don't want to try to relate with Me during their physical life, because it is too much of a headache. They therefore create many ideas of why it is not necessary to think about a God who lives in the sky. For example, they may say that if God does exist, they will find out what they need to do after they pass on to the next life.

Based on their philosophy, Lisa, these people feel your desire to relate with Me is unnecessary. But I can tell you, the reason parents want their children to grow is because they know that the best moments of relationship are when the children become adults, like them.

So, any person who considers he can stay like a child until he passes to the next dimension, will surely discover when he arrives that he cannot relate with Me.

Lisa: My God, I remember thinking that way, but I want to

be different now. I don't want to wait until the last minute of my life to see what will happen.

God: If I can make some comment to you, I want to recognize you have changed in comparison to what you used to know and to feel about yourself. I only hope you will not become content with what you have just started to achieve in your journey.

Lisa: I have to admit it is sometimes not easy for me to listen to You. I am very surprised that I feel this way, because I listen to many people, at my job or when I go out with my friends, and I seldom feel it is hard to listen to them.

God: I do think the process of listening to Me is like taking a wire that is thick and stretching it until it becomes very thin. That transformation is surely not pleasant. But, one thing is sure, the thinner the wire, the easier to transmit through it.

Lisa: Well, listening to You really stretches my mind. I think this is because what You speak about has all kinds of dimensions that I, and probably many other people, seldom think about.

God: In spite of your difficulty, will you consider continuing to listen to Me or will you abandon Me because it is too stressful? This is the reason I will say, listening to what I have to say is like a journey, because it brings you from one point to the next point.

But the most difficult thing for Me, throughout My existence, is to work with the same person without being abandoned along the way.

Lisa: I do want to continue to listen to You. And I would like

Fourth meeting

to say that in the midst of the difficulty to listen to You, there is also an aspect of excitement. You bring so many ideas that never occurred to me. You show me dimensions of such depth and profundity, really different from what I discuss with my friends.

God: Oh yes? My words have an emotional effect on you? I was thinking I was only introducing you to some new thoughts.

Lisa: Yes, Your words, especially when I accept them, create an emotional effect that I like very much. This is the main reason I like to listen to You.

God: So, after all you have experienced, can you consider believing I am with you, or next to you, or you are in My universe? In other words, do you feel from now on you will live your life without denying that I can be with you?

Lisa: Even considering the short time I have spent with You, I feel it would be hard to live without You from now on. I remember when I was a young girl, I did have the desire to speak with You, or at least to know if You existed somewhere. And now, You have given me so much more.

God: So, do you want to say to Me, Lisa, your life on this Earth can no longer be lived without My presence? Is this correct?

Lisa: Knowing what I used to consider as being important in my life, I'm surprised to find myself saying to You that it would be painful to live without You.

The Rebirth of God and Lisa

God: What about other people? Do you think it is acceptable for them to just live off the energy that is produced by the system of the natural world, which actually was created by Me, and yet not develop the dimension of their personality that will permit them to perceive My existence and to relate with Me?

Lisa: Well, My God, I do think we can be satisfied with the energy we receive from eating and sleeping, and whatever else we do, especially if we do not have any concept of Your dimension.

God: So, you think that this behavior or tradition that just sustains the human flesh can satisfy human beings.
  Yes, it is true, there is an energy within every particle of matter inside the human flesh. This energy has the ability to maintain a certain amount of space within that matter, and that space removes any pain that could be caused by friction between the particles. Is it because human beings don't feel any friction within themselves, that they are satisfied with their physical existence?

Lisa: If I just look at people's appearance, I can conclude that the degree of energy they receive from all the things they consume does satisfy them. But if there is an opportunity to have a conversation with these same people, the conversation will often turn towards the many reasons why they are unsatisfied.
  Therefore, to more fully answer Your question, all this energy that supports our bodies is far away from truly satisfying us.

God: So, if people are not satisfied, how is it possible they

Fourth meeting

can live unfulfilled and incomplete for so many years of their lives without rebelling or trying to find a solution? I can see they are trying to find solutions when there is a lack of food or a lack of resources for their many fundamental energy needs.

So, how come they are not desperate to find solutions for their feelings of being unfulfilled? Do they feel they need to keep a low profile because they have an agreement with someone or something that requires them to maintain their belief in the importance of secular pleasure only?

Lisa: I don't know how it's possible we can live this way, but I also lived this way for so many years until just recentgly when You came to visit me. Only now do I begin to realize there is another energy that exists besides the one we use in order to survive on a daily basis.

God: Indeed, it appears that you can live without My presence or the energy you can receive from Me, and pass your days just receiving energy through eating food, going shopping and so forth, for the sustenance of your flesh. But by only focusing in that direction, you will not be able to find your internal self who, through the process of its development and growth, is made to relate with Me.

Lisa: It looks like we can go on for quite a while without finding ourselves.

But the truth is, it is like a bad dream to live this way, something I was not aware of until I experienced the feeling that Your presence creates in me. This is the major reason I want to live with You from now on.

God: So, Lisa, what is the effect in you, when you go to work and fulfill your everyday duties without Me, in comparison to

The Rebirth of God and Lisa

living with the consideration that I am with you?

Lisa: I'm not so good at explaining, but I will try. Without You, we feel we are pushing ourselves, somehow passing through each day. In other words, it is a long day and we are only thinking of taking a break, catching our breath, or getting some energy from somewhere, like eating or drinking.

I'm not sure if You can understand what I am talking about.

God: It sounds to Me that human beings who live without Me are always pushing or dragging themselves, and I do believe this way of living must require a lot of willpower and determination, for the ones who have those qualities. And, by looking at this situation, I presume human beings must indeed be very tired at the end of such a day, as you imply.

But if this is what I created, surely I must be a God who is more concerned about creating human beings to suffer, than to see them happy.

Lisa: I'm not sure why, but every morning it is tough to get up and to get ready for the day. During the week I make a schedule to wake up one hour before leaving my home to make sure I look decent for my job. I feel that throughout the day I'm always looking for energy, and even the weekends can drag, for whatever the reason.

God: But didn't I hear from you, Lisa, that recently you have been learning to think about Me and to be grateful? Therefore, you should no longer have this problem of not having enough energy, right?

Lisa: Yes, I do think about You from time to time, but many times I still feel my body is heavy and I am just dragging it

Fourth meeting

along, trying to find reasons to make it move.

God: Can this be the reason you are interested in finding Me and relating with Me? Can it be because you want to change the heaviness that lives within you each day? Is it because you now know that if you don't relate with Me, your loneliness can become heavier than the weight of your body?

Lisa: Yes, it seems like this is my major motivation at this time.

God: So, Lisa, it looks like you are actually not interested in Me, but only in the energy that composes the Me!

Lisa: Well, maybe so, but to be honest with You, My God, I have a hard time to think of You any other way.

God: I now understand your motivation for wanting Me to live with you. It seems you wish that I would help you to have a day of lightness instead of a day of heaviness. In other words, you hope My presence will remove the feeling that causes you to have days where you drag yourself along.
    Is this the way you perceive I should be for you?

Lisa: It seems that You are not happy about my perception, but I'm not sure what I can do about it. Your energy has been motivating me to try to relate with You.

God: Personally, as your future God, I understand the difficulty of living without Me and why you therefore would want to receive a different feeling from Me, a feeling with the potential to transform the flatness of your everyday reality.
    So, I must make the conclusion, the reason you want Me as

The Rebirth of God and Lisa

your future God is so I can perform a magical transformation of everything you do not like into something you do like.

Lisa: Well, if there is something different I should be looking for, please let me know. But the fact is, before I met You and received Your energy, I felt like my days were so routine. People sometimes say that we are like machines, that's all.

God: So, the reason you want Me to be close to you is because you want to add some lightness to your day or some good feeling, when usually there is no feeling, so you will no longer experience a heavy or a boring day? Is this the truth?

Lisa: I think You are correct. But I also feel that I wish to end each day with the feeling that the day had some higher value, regardless of what I did or what I went through.

God: That is a good desire, Lisa. But if you want to feel value at the end of the day, or be recognized as a valuable person, you have to begin to see life around you differently. For example, look at the way art lovers observe a valuable painting.

What is interesting about these people is, they first try to observe what the painting means for them or has meant for others. Based on their research, they give a certain value to that painting, and they respect it more deeply. What is most interesting is that through their deepening relationship with the painting, they themselves can feel more elevated.

Until you learn about all of My dimensions, and begin to value each one of them highly, your wish to become valuable cannot yet be considered.

Lisa: Does this mean I have to choose a specific thought toward You if I want to create higher value? Isn't this what

Fourth meeting

people call a belief in something?

God: If you value Me just as a Being from whom you can take energy, like extracting oil from the land of the Earth and pumping it inside your car to power the engine, you can indeed consider this to be a great idea, if this is all you can recognize.

But if I say to you today, I am also supposed to be part of your life, as you are supposed to be part of My life, then your previous thought will be considered to be of low value.

Lisa: If I understand something, I should try to recognize a higher thought from, can I say, a lower thought, and if I can create a relationship based on that higher thought, I will acquire more value. Is this what You mean?

God: Throughout history, the most difficult thing for human beings was to accept a new idea with higher value, because they coudn't yet perceive any substance behind it. Because they could never find the substance until the idea was fulfilled, they always felt the idea must not be right, but instead must be wrong.

Therefore, human beings, with their full strength, usually try to demolish any new idea. But what they don't know is that there must be some substance before an idea can even arise. If they knew that law and valued it, the evolution of humanity would have taken only a few years.

Lisa: Then can I conclude, if a person who receives a higher thought doesn't value it, that thought can be easily destroyed, either by himself or by someone else?

God: If you observe yourself today, concerning what I tell

you, you will realize the most difficult thing is to believe what I say. When you don't believe in something, then automatically the word given to you is impossible to remember or to be printed in your mind.

As well, even if you do believe in My words for a short time, if someone later on convinces you that My words are not correct, that event will erase the words you used to believe.

Based on this reality, you can easily understand why it takes human beings such a long process through history just to learn such basic concepts as why they are born, what is the meaning of what is around them, and so forth.

Lisa: It's fascinating to see how everything that seems to us to be so philosophical, especially concerning the question of the purpose of life, seems to You to be so logical and to operate according to precise mechanisms. It almost seems that the concept of believing in You would no longer be necessary, because You bring more of a sense of proof.

God: In these days, human beings have a high desire to observe everything I created. I guess they are checking whether I made some mistake in mathematics, or created a wrong chemical composition.

But actually, in the midst of doing that, they are uncovering the secrets of how My mind functions. Because My mind is logical, when I talk to you it is difficult for Me to speak in a confusing way or in what your people call, a philosophical or a spiritual way.

Lisa: Oh, I see. But I would never imagine that to find Your presence in our lives, we would first need to take a science class to discover the mechanism of how everything works.

Fourth meeting

God: If human beings were more adventurous in accepting ideas and would then try to build the substance around these ideas by acting upon them, they would discover the main reason to be on Earth is to fulfill ideas, instead of questioning ideas, or rebelling against ideas, which they have all done.

But because of that, they could never build anything that could endure and could be pleasant to be around.

Lisa: Oh, I don't have any intention of rebelling against Your ideas!

God: I can see you are starting to think well. I will still ask you a question regarding your desire to find more energy. Do you think I feel interested in coming close to you just to give you energy? Or, do I hope you will accept My thoughts and value My presence, to the point every action you take will be in consideration of what you value?

Lisa: Well, to be honest, I can feel that my reasons so far do not make You happy. So, I hope to find the reason that will make You feel interested in coming close to me.

God: It seems you start to realize that you will need to have a profound purpose in order for Me to want to be with you. I can use an example from the animal world. When you observe animals, you realize that regardless there are so many kinds of animals living in the same territory, each kind knows with whom they should associate.

So, because I am God, any being who tries to relate with Me must first be qualified to relate with Me, or to be perceived as My creation. That being will need to resemble Me, not only by his or her form, but by his or her internal qualities as well.

The Rebirth of God and Lisa

Lisa: Yes, my God. I now realize You exist as Your own Identity and You do not have to respond to every demand we have, like wanting to receive energy. I can also perceive that You have a remarkable mind and, in order for me to relate with You, I have to develop my understanding of Your value.

God: To end My conversation with you, I will say, every wish human beings have pursued can be correct, according to the time and the place. But what is most valuable to Me is whether they are achieving the full potential for which I originally created them. If they can achieve this, surely they will not have difficulty to testify that I am with them.

Lisa: Thank you, my God, for coming to visit me this time.

God: Good-night, Lisa.

FIFTH MEETING

The Rebirth of God and Lisa

It had been a difficult day. I don't know if my work was the cause of my stress or if I just overall felt something was missing. The fact was that I didn't feel good about myself.

So, I decided to take a walk in the park to breathe some fresh air and to look at the leaves that were changing color. And, honestly speaking, the air made me feel better. It was pleasant to see all the dark trunks contrasting with the brightly colored leaves that were falling from the branches, part of the cycle of life.

Surprisingly, after I came back home, God started speaking to me. This event drastically changed my earlier uneasy feeling.

So, today I invite you to read that dialogue with God. I hope it will raise your feelings and lead you to a more profound understanding of your life, as it did for me.

God: Today I came to see you because I perceived you were alone and in a position where you were waiting for something or someone to come to you. Now, are you happy that I came?

Lisa: I am surprised that You could reach me today, but I am so happy You are here! I don't know how it is possible for You to come, because I didn't feel well today.

God: When human beings don't feel well, it means they had

Fifth meeting

a day that didn't satisfy them, but that doesn't mean it was a bad day for Me. Whatever you went through, even though it didn't feel peaceful to you, this situation allowed Me to perceive that your spirit was looking for something.

Maybe you do not know, but for the spirit to become more dominant than the reality of the physical existence, the best environment is when a person has difficulty in controlling his day or, in simpler terms, if this person has a tough day.

In this event, the secular matter takes a more objective position and therefore the spirit can be more subjective. And because of this reality, it is a good moment for you to become aware of what is happening with your spirit. This is the reason I said, a bad day for you does not necessarily mean a bad day for Me.

Lisa: So, if I want You to come every day, I should always have a bad or a difficult day?

God: If I answer your remark simply without being too precise, I will say yes. When human beings are too secure in what they do or too safe within their environment, there is no way they can perceive their spirit is demanding something. Thus, it is next to impossible for Me to meet their spirit.

This is the reason throughout history, a person who had the most chance to experience My presence was usually, if not all the time, a person who had a difficult life in terms of the physical aspects. But if you were to meet and to listen to this person's words, you would perceive that he had acquired wisdom through his life.

Lisa: How is it possible You can more easily perceive our spirit when we are struggling with physical things?

God: In the moment you struggle there are two major parts that separate themselves within you. One is an element of the spirit and the other is an element representing the body. If the spirit of a person is developed enough, I can in that moment come and infiltrate some element of Myself, hoping the person will take seriously what I introduce and use it to continue his or her development.

Lisa: I think I understand something, and I certainly appreciate that You could come to visit me today, due to my difficult day.

God: One thing you human beings never comprehend is, the angle you see life from will depend on what you consider to be a priority, which is usually what you perceive first. Therefore, since human beings first perceive their flesh, they tend to most highly value their flesh and consider this is all they have to take care of. But if they could change their angle and see from My viewpoint, they would see their spirit first. Therefore, they would consider taking care of their spirit as their first priority.

Until human beings change the angle of their viewpoint, they will never agree with what I say as needing to be valued first. As well, I will never agree with them concerning what they value first.

Lisa: Well, God, Your concept of what we choose as a priority is logical. It must be quite difficult for You to make us want to choose what You consider to be Your first priority, when we feel the need to take care of physical matters first.

But I also am aware that what I have chosen as my first priority throughout my life could have been my second priority, if I had made more effort to listen to my internal side.

Fifth meeting

God: I wonder if you fully comprehend what you are saying now, because you usually seem to have a clear philosophy about what you should or must do, as well as what other people should or must do. And, based on this philosophy, a certain aspect of your life has been prosperous.

But now, it looks like you are pushing away what you used to consider as valuable, and choosing to value developing your spirit instead, in order to grow your ability to achieve a connection with Me.

Lisa: Do you know, it's interesting that I start to see what I have achieved materially and intellectually, and it no longer contents me.

God: So, what do you think can make you content?

Lisa: I studied at school for quite a few years, about history, literature, philosophy, and many other things. Then I tried to achieve some independence through getting a good job and my own apartment. And that, for awhile, made me content

But now, I start to re-evaluate everything I experienced in the past, based on what You have taught me. I think what will make me happy today is to take the same amount of effort I have used in my life so far, and use it to meet You and to relate with You.

God: I am very pleased to hear about the possibility that My presence might become a part of your life, and that you would like to begin to learn something about Me.

Lisa: Actually, I didn't think that there was something that could please You. I was thinking that since You already have everything, what could I give to You that could have the power to make You happy?

God: So many times, I hear human beings trying to figure out what I am. They come with many ideas, and some are very close to the reality. And I am pleased with that. When they discovered I am omnipresent, that was absolutely correct. A second quality they discovered was that I am eternal. They were also well-informed concerning that idea.

What they didn't like to identify in Me was when they realized I could be smart, or very smart. They neglected to recognize that characteristic, maybe because they didn't want Me to become human, like one of them. As well, they had difficulty to acknowledge My intensity, maybe because they were not yet fully prepared to meet Me.

If human beings were to learn about every part of Me, they would realize I gave these same aspects of My character to them, too, in order that My knowledge could be perceived by them, and that My intensity of brightness could be absorbed inside of them.

Lisa: Oh, I think I would like to have Your brightness inside me!

God: However, there is a slight problem to achieve that.

Lisa: Oh, really?

God: Many times I see devoted people trying to pray or to talk to Me. But they are not concerned about creating possibilities where I can come close to them. And, because they do not check this aspect, what they do is useless.

Lisa: Me, too, many times I called Your name recently, but

Fifth meeting

I didn't feel You were with me. Yet at other times I could feel Your presence. Through that I do realize how difficult it is to bring Your presence, as well as to have confidence You will stay with me.

God: If I explain the main pathway to communication with Me, I will say the first intention human beings should have is to create a character that can resemble Me. Until human beings undertake to transform and re-create their character into what I consider to be suitable, whatever they do will be in vain, and therefore, they will never come to the point of creating a relationship with Me.

Lisa: Now that You say this, I realize it's similar to relating with people. When someone has a similar education as I do, I feel closer to him or her than to someone else who doesn't have the same background as me.

Does this mean I need to have the same knowledge as You have in order to begin to relate with You?

God: If human beings like you, Lisa, want to relate with Me, they must have some kind of minimum comprehension of who I am and what I am concerned about. By accepting to learn about some aspects of Me, they make the minimum base to begin a relationship with Me.

But there is a fundamental concept created by human beings concerning Me that hinders this relationship. That concept is that I do not feel anything or have any wishes. I guess that human beings feel that if I had feelings or wishes, I would be human, and no longer divine.

But they should consider, how can a child comprehend his or her own parents, if that child believes he or she should know nothing about the parents? Can we consider that son or daughter to be an adult, or just a child maintaining a wish to stay a child for as long as possible?

Lisa: Yes, it makes sense that a child should eventually learn about his or her parents' situation. But I have a question. I'm a person who reads a lot to make sure I'm knowledgeable, so I can better relate with people. But sometimes, after discussing with someone all there is to say about a certain field, we come to the point where we no longer have much to say to each other. Therefore, it seems that kind of relationship is also limited, isn't it?

God: Um, I see.

Lisa: The reality is that after a certain amount of time, I start to be bored with my relationships, and that feeling affects my attitude. It can get to the point that I feel unsure if I want to meet someone again. This kind of experience has led me to believe that something is missing in relationships.

God: Do you give this example from your life because you are afraid your relationship with Me will turn out the same way after you learn all that I have to tell you?

Actually, I am happy to hear your remark about exchanging knowledge between humans, and coming to a moment when you feel you no longer know how to communicate. I will also say to you, if human beings aquire knowledge about Me, this same reality will eventually occur. This is the reason I had to think about what should be created next, in order for a relationship to exist for eternity.

Lisa: I'm not sure what will happen if I gain a lot of knowledge about You. Right now I just want to explain what

Fifth meeting

I have experienced with friends of mine. We were close during the time we were studying or working together, but we became distant when we moved to different schools or jobs.

God: There is a saying in your world, Lisa, something like, birds with the same feathers, flying together. When you look at the birds flying over your head, you will see they do not mix with other kinds of birds. They only relate with the ones that look similar to them. Therefore, if you want to relate with Me, you first need to gain knowledge about Me. But knowledge is not enough by itself to build a relationship with Me.

Lisa: Does religious thought or do certain kinds of philosophies reveal knowledge about You?

God: Yes, I consider that to some degree many human beings have discovered various understandings about Me, even though many of those understandings have not been precise or clear. And unfortunately, because of these ambiguities, many humans have considered all this knowledge about Me to be something that could be discussed, argued about, questioned, or even dismissed.

Due to this situation, everything people discovered that could perhaps seem to be what I wanted to say became broken, demolished, and dismantled, to the point everything became relative and nothing was considered absolute. And because of that, many human beings began to feel that everything that had to do with Me was too confusing, and preferred to study the knowledge of what you call science, because they felt more secure and content.

Many religious people have felt, tragically, that if they study science they will find themselves going away from Me, whereas actually, they can become closer to Me through at least understanding the mechanisms of the universe, which is My creation.

But many people pursuing scientific knowldge have made one simple mistake when they were trying to discover the logic that sustains matter, which was that they removed Me as the Origin. They therefore became the enemies of the religious people who, even though their ideas were complex and confusing, did at least believe in Me.

Lisa: Personally, I have not had good experiences with religious people. They have a tendency to believe the knowledge they have about You is the only truth. It's difficult to discuss with them because my thought needs to fit so perfectly with what they say in order to be accepted by them.

God: I hear your point. From where I am, I do not look at human beings based on their knowledge. I look at them based on the quality of goodness of their spirit. Therefore, to achieve that goodness, I give knowledge to them so they can grow their spirit. Based on that, I try to have a relationship with them according to the development of their spirit, not according to their knowledge. But I use the mind of human beings to communicate My knowledge, which I do consider to be a necessary prerequisite to receiving the utmost from My presence.

If people knew that knowledge is only connected to their mind, not their spirit, they would accept to recognize the mind as only a place where knowledge is exchanged. Therefore they would not value being knowledgeable as the most important thing, especially if they want to communicate with Me. Instead, they would value their spirit as the core of their essence that permits them to communicate with Me.

Fifth meeting

Lisa: It's true, we human beings tend to believe that because we have knowledge we can relate with each other. Therefore, we are eager to check whether other people understand what we are talking about. If they do, then we think that we are in a relationship.

But what You're saying, God, is that You make a distinction between sharing knowledge and having a relationship.

God: To explain My point in more detail, I will ask you to look at yourself. You will see that each part of you has a different function. For example, your mind is made to register words and knowledge, whereas your spirit has other roles like breathing My air and receiving My energy.

Lisa: Can I say my mind is capable of acquiring knowledge and explaining it to someone who doesn't know it?

God: I think your explanation is very good. Are you describing what you do, and is this the reason you can explain it so well?

Lisa: Well, I didn't finish everything I wanted to say. I wanted to ask You if our spirits are made to receive Your energy and transmit it to someone else?

God: Yes, I am content with your explanation. For Me to come close to someone, I need to sense a spirit. When I sense a spirit, in that moment I am attracted to it and I can give My energy, which I am made of.

As your physical body is made to receive air and exhale it, your spirit has the same function. The spirit constantly inhales and exhales energy, if it is developed enough. But if the spirit is in an undeveloped stage, it is immensely incapable of doing that. I consider this stage as not having any relationship with the energy that I always exhale.

Lisa: I think now I'm clearer about what You're saying. Knowledge is knowledge and spirit is spirit. Each one has a different function. And, for You to have a relationship with me, I need to create my spirit so I can inhale Your energy.

God: Every time someone, or you, invites Me to come, that makes the spirit more subject toward the body. And because of that, I am capable of transmitting My energy, which is called love. But in the moment you stop turning toward Me, I can no longer perceive your spirit and therefore, I cannot relate with you.

Lisa: I'm really grateful to know what You need in order to meet me. I also start to realize that without Your energy, or love, inside of me, I can only talk with people about my knowledge, but I cannot have a relationship with them, because I cannot feel love for them.

God: Lisa, you really start to understand. If I were a God consisting only of knowledge, and only concerned with imparting My knowledge, then a long time ago I would have explained everything to human beings like, for example, what they needed for their physical survival. After that I would have left humans alone with all that knowledge.

But the reason I come to you, Lisa, is because I am interested in relationship and not just in knowledge. And a relationship of love is impossible to create alone, because someone else is always needed in order to know whether love is present. This is the reason I did not leave human beings.

Fifth meeting

Lisa: Sometimes people have told me, quite timidly, that they somehow wish to have a relationship with God, or they wish that God would guide them. Now I understand that we are all somehow longing for a relationship with You, for the purpose of experiencing love.

God: It looks like I have changed the focus of your being. Before you used to value matter the most, then I led you to the discovery of knowledge about Me, which interested you very much. Now it looks like you will agree with Me that discovering love can be much more exciting than anything else.

Surely, you are traveling at a high speed through many centuries of discoveries.

Lisa: Yes, it seems so. I realized that You were a God of knowledge because You released so much knowledge to me. But today You opened a new desire within me, a desire to find You and to have a relationship with You based on love instead of only knowledge.

God: I think you have a good amount of sincerity within you, which allows you to take the high speed road. Unfortunately, because not so many people came forward to tell Me what they felt after I spoke to them, human beings chose the most complex road, which took many generations, regardless each time I came to visit an individual, he or she must have experienced exactly what you experience now.

Lisa: Not long ago I believed that I knew something about life, and I thought that was enough for me to manage. Then, after You came to visit me, I thought I understood something about You, and that therefore I was having a relationship with You. But today I accept that to know something about You doesn't mean I am in relationship with You.

God: I think the difference between knowing about Me and having a relationship with Me starts to be clear to you. And I would say it is time for you, as well as for many people, to make a relationship with Me, if you want to experience what I originally planned for human beings.

Lisa: Yes, I hope this is the time for that, and I would like to be a part of that.

God: I want to tell you one more thing. I accepted to release My knowledge to people so they could understand Me intellectually. Based on that, I hoped they would begin to discover they could make a relationship of heart with Me.

But so many times they chose to believe that knowledge was the almighty achievement, and they elevated their view of themselves, to the point of believing they were superior to others. They even felt justified to destroy any human being who didn't bow down to their knowledge, or who valued love as more important than knowledge. And that really hurt Me, more than you can know.

Lisa: Well, I certainly don't want to do that! Even though human beings have a lot of knowledge, we need to concede it's not enough to begin to relate with You, because we are so lacking in the quality of love!

God: So, are you now going to reject all the truths you already learned, because you have discovered knowledge cannot be used to relate with My heart?

Fifth meeting

Lisa: I'm not sure what I should do. I guess I shouldn't reject what I have learned. But as You have made me understand now, knowledge is just knowledge. From now on I want to learn to have a relationship with You. Perhaps I can use my knowledge for that purpose.

God: I like your reasoning. It sounds mature and wise.

I can tell you, to start to learn about something that is not close to you, it is good to begin by learning about what is close to you. Is it easy to know about some country that is far away from you? No. It is after you have lived in your own country and learned its history and culture that you can begin to learn about another country. In the moment you start to discover there is knowledge, you can start to believe there is more knowledge to learn somewhere else.

Similarly, if you discover your potential to experience love, then you can start to believe that somewhere else, there is Someone who has love.

The question now is, what do you believe in at this point in your existence?

Lisa: My God, I appreciate what You tell me. I do start to discover my potential to have love. Maybe now I can help my friends, who study about all kinds of things, to not just acquire more knowledge to cover the feeling of being lonely or incomplete, as I used to do. I feel I now begin to perceive a higher level of value and I want to share this with them.

God: I am sad to see so many young people like you trying to find the fulfillment of their being through acquiring all kinds of information, and some of them studying so intensely. I think they believe they will find a treasure somewhere, instead of accepting that knowledge has an end.

 *The Rebirth of God and Lisa*

If they did accept that possibility, they would start to turn to Me to create a relationship of love, and they would discover fulfillment.

Lisa: Does this mean I can begin to share my life with You, even though in comparison to You I'm quite small?

God: Yes, Lisa, you can start to have a relationship with me, if you remember the only thing that gives value to you is the love you can receive from Me. This is a law.

Lisa: Thank you very much, my God!

God: Good-bye for now, Lisa.

SIXTH MEETING

Lisa: I miss You today, my God, and I am wishing so much to meet You.

God: Is it okay to wait a few minutes? I am in a conversation with someone else right now.

Lisa: Oh, You're here! Well, of course I can wait. But truthfully, it gives me a little shock to hear that You can be busy. I considered I was busy and this is why I didn't come for a few weeks.

God: Well, indeed, not so many people know My schedule. But also, nobody asks about My schedule. I guess no one is interested in it. Surely, they are more interested in what I can do for them.

Lisa: Oh, it's true, that kind of question didn't come to my mind. Perhaps it is because we are afraid to know something more in detail about You, in case Your response might oblige us to change something in our lives.

God: Thank you to inform Me why human beings never ask Me anything about My life, but instead are just involved with their own lives. And then sometimes I hear a scream, "Why don't You help me?" or, "Why did You abandon me?" Finally, after a while, I no longer hear anything. This is pretty much what I experience with human beings overall.

Lisa: I'm sorry. If You need to be somewhere, please take Your time. I am going to wait for You and at the same time prepare my paper and pen.

God: I appreciate that you gather all your materials. I interpret

Sixth meeting

from this preparation that My word has some meaning for you.

Lisa: Your words are not only meaningful—I cherish them. I try to write down everything so that I can review them afterwards.

God: Based on what you express, I will interpret that you respect Me. Is this correct?

Lisa: Yes, of course. Actually, my true hope is that You would see this as an act of loving You.

God: It looks like you wish to relate to Me with something more than respect. I cannot discuss this subject right now as I am involved with someone else. This someone doesn't have much patience and may interpret My delay as meaning that I don't want to respond to him. If I don't answer him, he will accuse Me for not responding, and will eventually reject Me.
So I will excuse Myself.

Lisa's Comments

After this, I excitedly looked inside my desk to find my journal and some pens. I wanted to make sure I was well prepared to write down everything God would tell me, as well as my responses, so I could re-read them later.

I hoped I was ready for whatever He would say. From my previous experiences I knew it was very important to not have any concepts about what I thought I already knew, because that would make God leave. And if that happened, I knew I would be extremely regretful.

It seems that when God is with someone, it is the most crucial time of that person's life, like it was for me. After receiving God the last time I felt so amazed by what I had learned and also by the emotional effect His words had on me. They made me feel so light and clean, like I was swimming in a pool of clear, pure water.

At the same time I was shocked to feel all of this happening to me. No other event had ever produced such an emotional effect in me. It was so deep and lasting. Maybe through reading what God told me, this emotion can come to you, too. I hope so.

However, after that meeting I had been very busy for several weeks, and I had not sought out God. It was when I started to feel a deep emptiness that I tried to turn back to Him. Still, I had felt somewhat doubtful when I called whether God would come.

Ten long minutes had passed and I was wondering if God had put me on His reservation list. Then I felt a cracking sensation close to my head, as if somebody wanted to knock me down.

God: Did you feel the time was long after I left?

Lisa: Yes! One minute seemed to be ten minutes. And ten minutes seemed to be a hundred minutes.

God: What do you think could be the reason that your impression of time appears to have changed? Is time measured based on some instruments that human beings created to designate what is considered to be one minute, or one hour? Or, is the measurement of time based on whether there is no 'air' to breathe for human beings, or there is so much 'air'?

What is time? I heard there is a great discussion in the midst of your people. Did I create the universe in six days? Or did I create the universe in six or more billion years, according to your measurement of time? It seems to be a deep dilemma for your people, to know which truth is true, or which side is right.

Sixth meeting

So, I bring the question to you, was the time long when I was not here, or the time short when I was not here? What clock are you going to use to measure the time since I left?

Lisa: I believe it was the anticipation of meeting You that made the time long. And, as I was anticipating meeting You, all the memories of the past meetings with You came back to me, and I wanted to see You so much. Then I started to feel the time became long, to the point every second became so slow, like the clock was ticking ten times slower than normal.

God: Yes, during the time you were preparing everything, in that moment your desire to meet Me started to open your heart, and that event created a sense of amplifying the time. This is the reason you perceived the time to be long. But when your heart is closed and you don't have any desire to find Me or to receive Me, the time can come and go and you don't perceive it.

So, I think your heart is open to receive Me now, isn't it, because the time appeared to be long?

To answer the question about which clock I used for creating the universe, if you measure time according to a mechanical concept, six or more billion years looks correct for the time I needed to create the universe. However, if you could imagine My excitement in creating the universe, the time would appear to be so short, as if it took only six days.

Lisa: Wow, thank you to explain that! It's true, there are a lot of arguments here about that topic. And yes, I was deeply anticipating the moment of meeting You, and I appreciate very much that You came.

God: What can it be that you appreciate so much?

Lisa: I appreciate the feeling I receive from You. It seems that only feelings make me discover who I truly am. It's important for me to find out who I am. So far, I have believed that through being responsible at my job and trying to relate well with my friends, that I could discover my identity.

God: So, did you find your identity? Many times throughout My existence I have heard people wanting to find their identity or their destiny, or to find themselves in the midst of all selves. It is like a collective voice screaming out from this planet Earth.

So, I have tried to approach this clamor and I have always wanted to ask, why do you scream? Why don't you look at what you have first, and appreciate what you have first? Everything is written in you, just not yet believed or not yet developed. If you can read yourselves, then you will know your destiny.

To give an example, if one day you hear your stomach screaming to your ear, what is my purpose, or, why am I where I am in your being, won't you want to tell it that first it has to believe it is a stomach and accept its role as a stomach?

Lisa: Well, that makes sense. But I did believe I had found my identity through realizing that I could manage an office. I could say, this job made me feel I had really achieved something in my life.

I was also satisfied with being independent and with feeling I could buy what I wanted, without needing to budget my money for several weeks or months. And most of the time I felt pretty happy being among my friends. But now, there is something else.

God: What can it be?

Sixth meeting

Lisa: If I am sincere with You, the reality is that only when I meet You and allow You to be with me, do I feel a sense of peace growing inside and around me, making me feel as if I were suddenly special.

God: But don't you perform a lot of secular achievements in order to feel special? Or, don't you become special just because you believe you can achieve something? At what moment do you recognize the achievement of a special feeling?

Lisa: It's a great feeling to walk through the middle of your workplace and feel every eye looking at you until you reach your office. But then when you sit down at your own desk, there is no more feeling of being special.

God: Oh, yes? Why is there no more feeling of being special? Is it because you created your 'specialness' based on a momentary event? Or did you create your 'specialness' according to something eternal? Which clock did you measure 'specialness' with?

Lisa: I don't know which clock I chose, but I do know, when people look at me, I feel I am special. But when I go inside my office, where the eyes of my colleagues are not focusing on me, everything that makes me feel I am special disappears.

God: So, based on what you tell Me, do you often go out from your office to be looked at, so you can feel your specialness growing again? Or instead, when you are sitting down in your office, do you hear the immense question, "What is achievement?"

Lisa: Well, those are a good questions. As I talk to You, I realize it's only when people look at me that I feel I have value. When I'm alone in my office, it is like my value disintegrates the moment I go inside. And, as You might know, we are many times alone, regardless we always hope to be seen by someone.

God: Well, if I were you, I would walk from the front door to my office and back again several times each morning to make sure people see me. What do you think about this idea?

Lisa: I think You're missing something, my God. If I did what You say, maybe ten times during the morning and another ten times in the afternoon, the people in my office would discover the reason I pass by is just to be seen. Then they would change the way they look at me and I wouldn't get the same feeling.

God: Oh, I see. Indeed, this is an immense problem in terms of feeling value from your achievements.

So, will you consider after your explanation, for an achievement to be special it must be so concrete and so real that it can be connected to something or to someone? And will you consider, as well, an achievement to be something we can relate with?

To give an example, look at the way the physical world is created. Is it an achievement, or is it not? If it were not an achievement, it means human beings would not be able to relate with what I created, they would not be able to use it or see its potential in relationship to them.

If I did create this physical world well, then it means you can relate with it, isn't it so? Therefore human beings can, at any place and by any means, relate with what was created.

Lisa: Well, Your answer seems a little complex to me, and all I can say is, it seems to be a nightmare to try to feel value. Do

Sixth meeting

You know, the purpose of all our hard work and sacrifice here is to achieve something so we can feel good about ourselves, like having a house that looks expensive or an apartment where there is someone to open the door for us. Feeling value is the main reason we like to be in charge of others, like I am at my office.

God: I think you must experience great difficulty in maintaining your value. And, I believe you must expend a lot of time and money to create an environment where someone can recognize you, or someone can look at you.

But do you know, if you achieve something that is connected to Me, I will also look at you? But this time, it will not just be for a short moment, but for a time that is immeasurable by your mechanical clocks.

Lisa: I will say yes, my main occupation is to always try to be looked at. And I think we also feel value from the little things we buy. In general, everything is motivated by our desire to feel good about ourselves. And I admit to You, it looks like we always need to do something or to buy something to have that feeling over and over.

God: It must be a difficult life to try so many times to feel value, like you said, and then, however good you feel about yourself, it can suddenly be burned to ashes. Do you think this is what I intended for human beings to go through and to always be vulnerable to?

Or, do you think I created human beings to know who they are, from the ends of their toes, to the top of their head, and from the surface of their skin to the deepest part of their being?

I will answer to you. I did not create human beings to be in turmoil, to never know who they are or what they are. Human beings have always had the ability to choose a special thought or belief that would allow them to feel happy, which distinguishes them as unique from all other creations. However, because they rejected this original thought, they, alas, chose momentary things that could only create feelings that stayed alive briefly.

Lisa: Yes, it seems like the feeling of losing our value threatens us, any time, any place. This is the reason we go to specific places, like certain stores or restaurants, for example, or even our office, to regain that feeling.

God: The solution for you, Lisa, is to have a feeling that can go inside you and maintain your value for today, tomorrow and at all times, isn't it?

Lisa: I would love to find that feeling, if it does exist. According to my experience, nothing has this ability, regardless certain things do provide some feeling of value for awhile.

God: Maybe it is normal to experience only a brief feeling of value from things that only contain a small quantity of energy or life within them.

Lisa: Maybe so, my God. But I would like to have a feeling that can maintain itself for a longer time.

God: Seen from a logical viewpoint, why should you get a long-lasting feeling from something that has a short life? For example, if you take some flowers into your house, how long will these flowers give you pleasure every time you look at them? It depends on the lifetime of those flowers.

If you buy clothing, which I believe you must do, how long

Sixth meeting

will this clothing make you feel you are special in it? There are so many factors that can destabilize this reality. One is whether the colors can be maintained as they were in the first place. Secondly is whether the form of the clothing can keep the same profile as when you first bought it. And thirdly is whether the ambience where you are wearing it now is equal to where you wore it before.

In the moment any of these things starts to deteriorate, then every feeling that was connected to these garments starts to also evaporate. This is the reason, I guess, you will discontinue using those clothes, regardless they did not yet arrive to the stage where you see holes in them.

Lisa: Because I like logic, then I realize how very logical You are in the way You speak to me, and I cannot deny what You say. But what I do not understand is, when I listen to those who believe they know You, why don't I see much trace of logic in their explanations?

How is that possible? Is it because You speak to them differently?

God: I will try to address that question later. As for your original question, if you use a battery that is made to store a certain quantity of energy within it, you know for how long you can pull out the energy from it. The bigger the battery in which you store energy, the longer your device can continue to function. But the solution to your demand for electricity is not just to store the energy in a limited area and place. The solution is to find the way to produce energy abundantly, so that people can use it to continuously brighten their whole environment.

So, based on the discovery of how energy is created, stored and disseminated, the environment of human beings has been brightened physically. Similarly, if human beings can discover a mechanism that permits them to receive the energy enabling them to be enlightened, they will be as bright as I am bright.

Lisa: That sounds very exciting! And, I can now see how useless it is to desire to have value when I have not yet created anything of real value, aside from my external achievements, which I can perceive through my paycheck or from the looks of my co-workers.

God: If you examine any desire of your being, nothing is incorrect. Every desire is correct. Each one is made so you can perceive what direction your being has to go. If your stomach is empty, it will tell you it has the desire to be filled. Similarly, if your mind wants to understand something, your desire to research this situation will be intense, and if you accept this desire, you will look for the knowledge that will satisfy it, even if it takes much time and effort.

Let's observe now your desire to be looked at, or to be liked. Is it a desire that should be suppressed or is it made to be fulfilled? Your desire will tell you if it is satisfied or not, or whether it feels full or not. If people look at you, and those looks do not satisfy your desire, it means you should not continue to focus in that direction. Instead, you should drive yourself to another place, to find something that can satisfy your desire.

Lisa: Why do we have this desire that everything around us should make us feel we are special?

God: If human beings were sincere, they would distinguish between the different levels of energy that can be produced. As you have experienced, there is energy created by things,

Sixth meeting

like clothes, and energy created by a look from someone. Do you see the difference?

Lisa: I do know, when I buy a suit for my work, there is a certain joy to buy it and a certain pleasure to wear it. I also know, when I come with my suit and people compliment me on it, that feeling can help me to be confident enough to handle the pressures of managing that meeting. Also I can see there is a difference between the feeling produced by buying a suit and the feeling produced by someone looking at me.

God: I think you are correct in the way you perceive these two distinct events.

Personally, when I created the universe, I created each element based on something lower than it and something higher than it, or something smaller and something bigger. Because of this hierarchy, every being knows to what place it belongs, based on what is above it and under it.

But when human beings came to be, something troubled them, to the point they no longer knew what was under them and what was above them, or what was smaller and what was bigger than them. And because of that, they no longer knew how to relate with whoever and whatever lived around them.

Therefore they started to use everything created around them for themselves, alone. And that created a huge chaos out of the order of My universe.

Lisa: Wow, it's a big thing to realize that because human beings do not know who they are and where they fit, the universe became chaotic. It is difficult for us to imagine we can be so essential, because we have the tendency to believe that we are alone. That is why we want to use everything around us for ourselves.

God: The reason I allowed the multitude of human beings to become more scientific in these days, rather than so religious like some time ago, is because I wanted them to discover the laws that permit the universe to sustain and maintain itself according to a certain order. Based on what they discovered, I felt they would be able to understand something deeper about My purpose in creating them, especially when they would discover that if one specific molecule or cell did not fulfill its role according to what was planned, this could destabilize the entire complexity of an object or an organism, or eventually the whole universe.

In other words, I wanted them to discover the most important law, that particles are intertwined with each other to the point they are part of the majesty of the whole universe. From the discovery of that truth, I was hoping that people would adopt this logic and accept this process that would also make them a part of the universe, especially concerning the realm of emotion.

But to do that, they have to accept that the realm of emotion is also created based on logic.

Lisa: God, it looks like You are not as preoccupied as I am to find value about Yourself. Instead, it looks like You are preoccupied with many other things that we human beings have difficulty to understand.

God: In some ways I do have very different preoccupations. This is because people have come to a point in their existence where their sense of how to obtain true value has become numbed, and because of that, they are constantly looking in every imaginable direction to find value.

Because they do not know with certainty or truly believe that I exist, they look toward what they can touch to find that

Sixth meeting

value. Due to that, I am always in pursuit of them, hoping they will recognize My existence as the source of their value, while they are always running away from Me, believing that is the way for them to find their value.

Lisa: What a dilemma! God, do You know that here we always want to solve mysteries, either in books or within ourselves? But surely we would never think that turning to You could be the answer to the biggest mystery, because many people have already believed You exist and yet we haven't seen an end to our problems.

God: Throughout My existence, I have initiated many geniuses by giving new ideas to their minds. I helped them to see things through inspirations or visions, concerning how My world is created. And many of these people tried to express to others what I led them to know, as keys to unlock the mechanisms of the universe.

But My investment remained hidden because it was invisible, to the point these people felt they were the creators themselves, or started to believe they knew everything. Although I inspired them, they removed Me as the Origin, which was very painful. And because of that, the mysteries of life were not solved, but continued to be mysteries.

But do you know that your people's dilemma is very similar to My dilemma? What good is it to be the Origin, if there is no physical manifestation of that Origin? Similarly, if you have a physical object but do not know the origin, then what good is it to have that object?

Until human beings choose by their own will to accept Me as their Origin, their lives will continue to be a mystery.

Lisa: I think human beings from the beginning have tried to find knowledge in order to solve life's mysteries. But I can see, as You mentioned a few times, that every time we discover something, we do not acknowledge You are behind it. Is this the major reason why we do not solve our problems?

God: Yes, I do remember every so often someone would come to talk to Me about their idea of what could be the meaning of life. But maybe because they felt I was not really there, they created many different thoughts. Or, because I didn't answer them the way they liked, they continued to create their own thoughts.

Then after some silence, I heard other people talking about what these thinkers had said, to the point they were considered to be the founders of a certain thought.

The tragedy is, if these thinkers had come to Me and put themselves in a place where I could communicate with them, I would have taught them the real thought that would permit them to find themselves as well as to find Me.

Lisa: Oh, I see. And yet, we really respect these thinkers here on Earth. Every time we encounter something mysterious or unknown, we look for an expert to help us determine what is going on or what is right or wrong. Usually we call this person a philosopher, a scientist, a doctor, a theologian, or some other name according to the field. But what we cannot know is whether this expert's knowledge is something created by that person himself, or if it really comes from You.

God: Did you find someone among your people who wrote some theory that could help you to find the element of life that could give you value for more than one day?

Lisa: No, I haven't found any writer or any thinker who

Sixth meeting

discovered that element. Maybe it's because we never asked the thinkers to think about that, or maybe it is because they don't know the answer.

God: I think they do not know the answer, otherwise I would know them. No one can know the answer to this question until they include Me in their conclusions.

Lisa: What do You mean by that?

God: There are certain things in this universe that were created a long time ago, like matter. But there are other things that can only be created during a person's lifetime. Acquiring physical things makes you feel special for a limited time because of the limited quantity of energy they are created with. And as well, knowledge, which is outside yourself, has to be learned and applied in order to promote a specific environment that can help you to enjoy a certain balance in your life. This knowledge liberates a quantity of energy that is greater than what physical matter can give to you.

But even knowledge is not enough for you to maintain your value for your eternal life. This is another dimension that has to be created in the midst of your physical life. This dimension has the purpose of giving you value that will maintain itself for the duration of your existence.

Lisa: Is this why we cannot feel so great regardless of what we achieve in our lives, like having a house or a car, or a job with prestige?

God: Dear Lisa, I think you are approaching a specific point of awareness in your life. If you look only to the physical world, there is no answer to satisfy your desire to feel value for more than one day at a time. This is the reason human beings began to discover the world of the mind. It was not just because they were looking for knowledge, but because they were driving themselves to find more value. This is why someone said, "Because I think, therefore I am."

Lisa: It looks like I'm in trouble, based on what You tell me, and I need to choose something new.

God: Do you experience something different when You meet with Me? Do you think I am like matter, or am I greater than what matter can be? Do you think I am equal with what knowledge can offer to you, or am I more valuable? Or, do you just think I am?

Lisa: I do experience something much more deep with You. Every time You come, I am amazed by what I learn from You, but even above that, I experience a lot of emotion in the midst of all the knowledge that You give to me.

God: Does this emotion satisfy your desire to become valuable, or does it make you want to leave and go somewhere else?

Lisa: At first, because I considered myself to be pretty knowledgeable, I was overwhelmed by the way You turned my mind in all different directions, to the point I could not but accept whatever You said to me. And I should confess, You have a really special style.

God: I have a special style? Or is it because you don't have so much experience with My way of talking, therefore you consider I have a special style?

Sixth meeting

Lisa: Yes, that's true, but especially I realized that when I started to accept what You taught me, many feelings began to appear. To receive so many emotions was something new to me and, as well, surprisingly pleasant.

God: You discovered you had feelings? Should I say to you, that is amazing, or should I say to you, what a tragedy!

Surely, throughout the history of My existence, the most difficult issue to make people aware of was not whether I existed somewhere in some corner of the universe, or even that I could be next to them sometimes, which they did to some extent recognize through words such as 'omnipresent' and 'omnipotent'. The real issue was that humans could not agree I was a God who had the character and the nature of love.

Because they did not recognize that, they could not imagine that someone on this Earth could feel My love. Therefore, any being who did feel love from Me was in danger of being destroyed.

Lisa: Well, I am obliged to recognize these feelings, because I feel different than usual, different than when I attend a meeting at my work or go out with my friends. When I meet with You, I'm surprised to discover the depth of my feelings.

God: So, you want to tell Me you experience many feelings from the way I talk to you? How is that possible? I was thinking a conversation is only intellectual.

Lisa: Yes, I am shocked, myself, to feel something, because I do consider our conversations to be quite intellectual.

God: And you have also realized, when you accept what I say, regardless you do not understand everything, you actually receive as well a certain quantity of energy that accompanies the words I give to you.

If people did agree with what I said to them centuries ago, they would have known that I was the God of energy, and the God of love. Therefore, they would have included that reality when they described who I was.

But because human beings were so defensive toward these feelings, for whatever reason, they preferred to reject My words, which meant they rejected My love. This is why no thinker wrote that I was a God of love.

Lisa: I think You are right. I did not connect the two together at first, but it is true, I feel good after I accept Your words. And, what is interesting is that I haven't felt the necessity to unburden myself to my friends as much, or to look around all the shops in my neighborhood, something I used to do quite often.

God: If I understand something, when I meet you, you suddenly feel value about yourself, correct?

Lisa: I think I'm obliged to say yes, regardless I'm afraid to, because I realize I need You to have value. You see, it's not so popular today to feel we need You, because we have worked so hard to gain independence from our parents, from our teachers, and from everything and everyone else as well. And of course, independence from You.

So, do you know, to be dependent upon You doesn't look like I am going forward, but going backwards.

God: Well, I am obliged to say that without Me you cannot have value. As well, it looks like you are obliged to say you need to be with Me to feel value.

Sixth meeting

Lisa: I remember You saying before that everything on Earth is already created with a certain energy capacity. Can value be something that is not yet created?

God: I am very pleased to see you are listening well and especially that you are remembering well.
  Now, will you accept the theory that value can only be created if you accept My presence to be with you? If you accept this theory, you will have to use it during the whole time your physical existence maintains itself, in order for you to gain the maximum amount of love before you mutate into another dimension, where the soul or the spirit exists. There, you will need to have a certain quality or substance of love in order to relate with Me and with other beings who have the same quality of love.

Lisa: I remember always wishing to feel valuable. But now, after listening to what You say about value, it seems that if I want to feel valuable for more than one day, it will take a big commitment, won't it?

God: I will say that this is correct. You can call the situation of Me being with you or you being with Me, a commitment. I will call it more of a communion because it is through the union of two parts that value is built and amplified. I know that in your world people haven't found this concept, but instead, some have theorized that when two parts reject each other, higher value is created or evolution occurs.
  But in fact, this theory of rejection brought human beings to the lowest level of their existence, to the point where their value became so unperceivable that they could hurt themselves and others without even knowing.

Lisa: Now I understand why You said You would know if someone had value, because according to You, to have value we need to live with You and You with us.

God: I am pleased to hear the way you comprehend everything. You are sharp.

Lisa: So, as I think more about it, this actually means I am obliged to have You with me, if I want to pursue my wish to have value.

God: Well, honestly speaking, you are not obliged to do anything. But if you don't integrate Me into your life, you cannot be more than you already are.

Lisa: Yes, my God, I agree, I am not obliged to do this, yet in some ways it looks like this is part of the deal in order to gain value. Still, I don't know if I am ready to accept completely. I don't see myself as a person who makes deals, but I also have to admit, to be just what I am is not acceptable. Maybe this is already the beginning of a deal.

God: When you go to a beautiful restaurant, do you accept it as part of the deal that you have to pay more because this restaurant produces a specific feeling, which the owner intentionally created?

Lisa: Yes, my God, I choose different restaurants exactly for what You said, for specific feelings.

God: Let Me choose another example. Let's say you go to a specific store and the people there have the talent for taking meticulous care of your particular needs. Will you agree this

Sixth meeting

specific place also produces a good feeling, and this is one of the major reasons you choose this store over other stores?

Lisa: Yes, now that You make me aware, I do realize many physical events produce feelings. Then the question is, do I accept how important these feelings are to my life?

God: Until you and human beings acknowledge the world of feelings without being afraid of them, the door to the most invisible dimension cannot be opened, and therefore I cannot be present. Until human beings accept to see their lives not just based on a material concept, or an intellectual concept, their lives cannot have value.

But when they decide, like you now try to decide, to accept that feelings are the most important part of them, then they will begin to know who they are, and as well they will discover that I was before everything began.

Lisa: Yes, God. This is why I still feel You are the God of 'somewhere' for me, because I cannot completely grasp the depth of Your feelings.

God: I am the God of 'somewhere' for You as long as I am not with you. But if you decide to choose Me, I will be with you, and you will know it, because your feelings of value will blossom.

Lisa: As You are speaking, I can perceive different emotions in me. Some make me feel You are very close and some make me feel You are far away.

God: If you become aware that My knowledge is created to guide you to the realm of emotion, you will surely be eager to distinguish the absolute truth from the absolute not truth, because when you align with the absolute truth, you will be able to come closer to Me, and therefore you will be able to feel Me.

But when you have the thought of absolute not truth, it will project you to a distance so far away, you will be obliged to reject My existence, and to even question whether you exist.

This is the reason I am always trying to give My word, to explain the closest understanding of what I am and why I created everything in order that humankind can become closer to Me, if they believe in My words. If this can be realized, then surely they will feel Me close to them, instinctively.

Lisa: So, if I am with You all the time, this will make me feel value all the time, not just for a few hours or for a day?

God: Yes. I think you start to understand that My words contain energy, and if you recognize them, you will also receive a feeling, and this feeling will help you to nourish the internal side of your being.

Lisa: Do You know, God, I've always been a person who looks for adventure by various means. For example, when I go to a party, I'm looking for an excitement that I expect the party will create. If I don't experience that excitement, then I don't recognize this party as being good. But even a good party doesn't have the power to sustain my sense of value for more than a few hours. I guess this is the reason I have maybe come to an end of looking for adventures.

God: I am pleased you accept to admit the feelings from all these different adventures do not last long, and at the same time do not satisfy the deepest part of yourself, which actually

Sixth meeting

is your soul.

Lisa: When You speak about the soul, it makes me remember that I was taught when I was young that eternal happiness comes from our soul.

God: If I may adjust the education you received from your former tutors, it is My presence inside your soul that makes it content and at the same time gives you the supreme value that you are looking for. It is not just because you are aware of having a soul that you will feel you are valuable.

Lisa: Then the question I should ask myself is, how can I make You want to live in my soul?

God: Yes, Lisa, your question and your desire are absolutely correct. Maybe you remember Me telling you that to achieve this you need to have the same nature as Me.

Lisa: Yes, my God. But many times it seems an impossible dream or even disrespectful to want to be like You. And I think many people on this Earth believe the same way as I do. It is considered to be arrogant, and because we don't want to be arrogant, we automatically reject any desire to acquire the same characteristics as You. But, I think we are confused.

God: I don't know what is happening in your physical world regarding your theory that says it might not be respectful to want to be like Me. I do know that if a seed wants to grow into an orange tree, it first needs to come from an orange tree. But if that orange seed says to itself it might be pretentious to want to become like an orange tree, I think that seed will not grow.

For what else can that seed do, if it no longer has any value or purpose, than to just accept to die?

Lisa: Yes, I guess it must be similar with us.

God: If a human being wants to feel ripe and juicy one day, it can only happen if this human being accepts to fulfill his or her destiny, through receiving the elements of life that will permit him or her to be nourished to the stage of becoming a ripened fruit.

If the plant world knows that, how come human beings do not know that? Is it perhaps because they do not want to become an excellent fruit for someone who wishes to taste them?

Lisa: Well, because we are all created by You, I would presume it should be a natural process to grow to become ripe and juicy, as You call it.

God: If what you say is true, that everything is created and raised by Me, then every seed should become a beautiful fruit. But the question is whether or not this is true for each child. Will each child grow up to become a beautiful being? If he or she does not, it means something else was influencing that child to not become a beautiful being.

Lisa: It looks like You don't agree with the belief that many people here have that we are created according to Your image. I thought that was what we were supposed to believe.

God: I will say to you, what you know is what you know, but what you don't know demands you to keep an open mind. If you compare everything that is new with what you already

Sixth meeting

know, you will never have new knowledge. Therefore, it will be impossible for you to become a new being.

As long as you are looking for something you do not know, and accept to learn it without checking what you already know, then you have a chance to change.

Lisa: Yes, my God, I do realize the difficulty I have to communicate with You comes from having a strong opinion about what I think I know. I can see that I always need to allow some space for You to say something I don't expect.

God: Indeed, this is the true attitude that will permit Me to communicate with you most easily. The reason I am able to talk to you is because you are not sure about everything. Therefore you are receptive at times, and this permits Me to speak to you according to your need. But the moment you consider you know without a doubt, you actually force Me to never come back to you, regardless it sounds like not having doubts is a great virtue for your people.

But for Me, it means I have to choose someone else who can allow Me to tell this person something he or she doesn't know yet.

Lisa: Your explanation makes me feel I'm not quite qualified to be in a dialogue with You, but at the same time I am very grateful that You can continue to come.

God: So, can you accept that every fruit can only become ripe and juicy because it is connected to a tree that is solidly rooted in the soil?

Lisa: Yes, of course.

God: And, if the fruit does not receive enough nourishment it will not reach its full potential of maturity and it will not please you, to the point you will not want to eat it as a dessert?

Lisa: Yes.

God: Then if human beings want to be ripe and juicy, or in their language, 'lovable', they need to be connected to a tree that is lovely. Will you agree with that?

Lisa: Yes. I like the images You create with Your examples, they make Your points become more real for me. I should use Your technique more often when I try to explain things to others.

God: So, can you agree that your mind is created with the same structure as My mind? Or, do you still prefer to say your mind is a product of your own effort?

Lisa: To be honest, I have always preferred to say my mind comes from me, because I like it when peole recognize my ideas.

God: How many people ask you where your ideas come from?

Lisa: Usually when I go to a meeting and give a report, a few people will approach me afterwards and compliment me on how well-organized I am, and how convincing my arguments are. In that moment I feel high value. But, to be sincere with You, I often don't give credit to the people who trained me, and I certainly never thought to give credit to You for the sharpness of my brain.

Sixth meeting

God: I can see your problem.

Lisa: However, I do start to realize one thing now. If I cannot find my value from Your presence with me, I will always need to find new people who recognize me, in order to feel a little bit of value.

God: If I understand something, are you saying you and your people are always trying to find value by exposing your talent to each other, hoping someone will make a remark to make you feel good?

Lisa: To be honest, I think You understand very well what I said to You, and I also feel You aren't impressed.

God: Well, I feel sad that the fruit doesn't know where it comes from. I think if a fruit could speak, it would never deny its tree, regardless the tree might not look important at first glance. A fruit absolutely knows its existence, its talent and its beauty come from the greatness of the tree. So, if I were impressed with your style of trying to find value, it means I would be denying the whole process of My creation. If I deny how human beings are built and why they are built, it means I also deny who I am.

This is the reason I cannot agree with everything, regardless many of your people who try to promote Me have said that I can accept everything. But the reality is not based on whether I try to accept everything, but based on whether the fruit a tree produces is desirable.

Lisa: It seems You are not impressed with us because You don't see us as being beautiful fruits.

God: Human beings maybe don't know, it is not because their physical self looks mature and complete based on their age, that they can please Me. It is only when a human being fulfills a level of goodness equal to what I can consider to be good, that I can start to recognize him or her as being the highest fulfillment of My creation. Similarly for a fruit, regardless how nice it can appear externally, if it does not arrive to the stage where it is absolutely sweet and desirable, that fruit cannot be recognized in the midst of the world of fruits.

Lisa: Yes, this is exactly my reality. Even though I look fine externally, I'm not happy with myself and I always find myself trying to get attention from the people around me. Maybe the reason I'm looking for recognition is because I'm not yet a being who can be recognized, what do You think?

God: Isn't your method time consuming? Doesn't it take enormous concentration to always be alert for the moment when someone will cross looks with you and recognize something about you, just so you can feel a little spark?

If you consider all your efforts to try to find someone who can applaud you, and if instead you were to transform those efforts into trying to develop your being to the stage where beauty becomes visible, you would not need to check whether people look at you, because they would automatically be attracted to you.

Lisa: I never considered that I was working that hard, but the fact is I always feel tired at the end of the day. I thought this feeling was only related to my work, but now I see that it's mostly due to my constant desire to be looked at and recognized.

Sixth meeting

God: So, I hope you will choose well what you want to become. But remember, whatever you choose, it is your choice, not Mine. If your choice allows you to meet Me again, then I will say you comprehended well what I came to tell you today.

Lisa: I think this is what I feel called to do. I want to take Your presence with me as something very serious and make it a priority in my life.

God: I think you choose wisely.

SEVENTH MEETING

Seventh meeting

I was glad when summer finally arrived. I like it when it's hot, because I can go swimming with my friends close to where I live. I truly enjoy swimming and being around water in general, with its special ambiance.

Still, this year was different from previous years. I realized I didn't enjoy as much some of the things I used to enjoy. Since my first meeting with God, I had felt out of place at times. Different situations that I had felt fine with before became difficult to relate to. For example, sometimes I used to go out with my friends and as we ate together we complained about our work or the people we knew, I guess believing we would feel better. Since God had given me His view, I didn't see those situations in the same way. When I tried to give a different point of view to my friends, they felt I didn't understand what they were going through.

But in spite of these experiences, overall I felt more peaceful. I believe it was because I felt somehow God was with me, even though I didn't connect with Him as much as I wished to. I got too busy with the everyday demands of my life instead of turning to Him in order to become 'juicy and lovely', as He would call it.

In less busy moments I would become aware of how much I missed Him and I found myself calling Him, hoping He would respond to me. It was not that I was praying to God in the conventional sense, but more that I was turning my thoughts towards Him.

After doing this many times, God did manifest Himself again to me. One thing I have discovered about God is that He always speaks as if He had never left me. He continues right where we left off at the last meeting. He also seems to know what has been happening in my life before I explain it to Him. This really amazes me.

God: Hello Lisa. Are you happy that I have come to visit you today?

Lisa: Yes, more than happy, I am truly excited to hear Your voice! Do You know, sometimes I feel I am just someone in the middle of the masses of people, trying to keep myself busy and productive. But the moment You come everything changes. Whatever was happening somehow disappears and to be with You is all that exists.

God: I thought you liked keeping yourself busy, trying to fulfill your aspirations. Have you been changing your interpretation of life since You met Me?

Lisa: Yes, I believe so. I can see I'm changing my way of thinking and my choice of words, almost without even intending to, and my priorities are different from the time I first met You.

God: Do you regret leaving your previous priorities of life behind?

Lisa: I will say it's surprising to see myself interested in something so intangible and changing my life accordingly. Before, I strongly believed the purpose of my life was being successful and independent. But since You came to speak to me, in those few meetings You could dissolve much that I believed to be so important.

God: If you knew how words were created, you would also understand how they can be replaced by different words. Words are just vocabulary created by your people to express something physical or metaphysical.

Seventh meeting

Therefore, if you have used a certain set of words to explain particular experiences in your life, and this explanation no longer fits with the reality of your life, you will usually reject those words or cease to believe in them.

But if I can instruct you with words that have the potential to explain your situation, you will want to identify with them. In addition, some words will show you something you can be, but are not yet. These words are made to help you to change your view of life, and demand from your part a new set of beliefs.

Lisa: If I understand what You are telling me, it means that before hearing Your words, my vocabulary was limited?

God: One thing is for sure, you did not have the proper view or understanding about your destiny, because you didn't have the proper angle to see your life. If you are inside of life, you see from inside of it, but if you are outside of life, then you see all the things that are around it. I am above life, and therefore I see everything.

Do you think a molecule knows what it is connected to? Or do you think you can see better what a molecule is connected to?

Lisa: I think I can see better from my viewpoint outside of the molecule.

God: That is correct, Lisa.

I have another question for you. Do you know why it is that human beings forget to come to Me to receive the food they need for themselves, regardless they feel lonely or a lack of energy?

Lisa: Maybe we forget to come to You because one thing or another preoccupies us.

God: I don't understand how You can forget about Me, since you are born from Me. Can you forget your parents who created you, or at least created your physical substance?

Lisa: Well, no, we don't forget our parents so easily, especially if they are good parents. Somehow we always find ourselves thinking about them, worrying about them and how they are doing. Also, sometimes we complain about them, because we wish to have something better than what we have, I guess.

God: What can be the reason you think about them if it is not because, every time you think about them, a slight bit of happiness is born within yourself?

Lisa: Hmm, I see. Then, if we don't want to think about our parents, is it because we feel some unhappiness when we think about them? Can this also be possible?

God: This is tragically correct. Therefore, for many millennia I have tried to introduce myself to humankind, hoping they would believe in Me and choose Me as their parents, so they could experience happiness and peace and all the other emotions that can be born inside of them if they decide to turn to Me.

One thing I think you have experienced. What happens when you go to the beach or someplace where you can face the sun? Do you think, when you face the sun, you become cold or you become hot? If you feel cold when the sun is supposedly hot, it is either because you are not honest about what you feel, or because the sun is actually cold.

If you feel hot when you are facing the sun, it is because the

Seventh meeting

sun must be hot. Whatever you face will always be reflected back toward yourself. So if you feel cold, it is because you are facing something cold, and so forth.

Lisa: So, because You are aware that there are not so many of us who actually have the kind of parents through whom we can experience complete happiness when we think about them, therefore You hoped we would turn to You. Is this correct?

God: This is a sad part of My history and the history of human beings. Initially I planned that every parent would turn out to be the most beautiful being existing on this planet Earth. But because the force of destruction got involved in the creation as well, My ideal was shattered and people were obliged to take the road of the one who infiltrated My creation.

Because of that event, people have been seeking the least valuable thing, which is to possess matter. Therefore, My only option was to find a way to make them aware that I do exist and have a plan for them. But the major difficulty was, and still is, that I am immensely invisible. But even so, I am not unperceivable.

Lisa: What do You mean by, You had an idea but something else got involved in the creation?

God: If you knew My original plan concerning human beings, you would know that a person who achieves goodness, as he or she is capable of achieving, will turn out to be so wonderful that the children who come from this person would only need to turn to their parent with open hearts, responding fully, in order to receive the elements of life. Then these children would themselves become the future parents, to the point that no one would need to go directly to Me, because when they look at their parents, they would see My goodness in them.

However, because this did not occur, I had no physical person through whom I could manifest Myself, and I was therefore obliged to try to present Myself without a physical form. Tragically, due to My invisibility, My journey to try to make human beings aware of My existence became a nightmare.

Lisa: If I understand something, can I say it was not Your original plan that we would need to seek You through religion or philosophy?

God: Originally, only the first human beings were, to some degree, faced with the difficulty to turn to Me. If they had done so, their hearts and all their qualities as human beings would have flourished. After that, every child would only need to think that their parents were the best parents in the world, and believe their parents were like Me, God.

Lisa: I think that the dream of every parent is that their children will be grateful to them and admire them at least, even if those parents don't quite believe they are the same level as You.

God: Yes, children were meant to admire their parents, who were supposed to have the same nature as Me. In this way the hearts of the children would be nourished. This is the reason I have asked you to admire and to recognize Me, so you can have food for your soul. If you do so, your heart will expand and grow like a mushroom bursting out from the ground after receiving a few drops of water to wake it up.

Lisa: I believe it must be sad for You to hear people rejecting

Seventh meeting

You or forgetting You, like I did all these long years.

God: What bothers Me is to see that human beings do not regard it as important to believe in Me. They feel they can easily reject Me because I am invisible. But the tragedy of this action is that their true selves cannot be born and develop through receiving the elements of life, which only I have. These elements would nourish the deepest part of their souls.

An interesting aspect about plants is that some require more of a specific mineral than another, and if they cannot find that mineral in the soil, they will not survive longer than a few days or weeks. It is similar to the soul, which demands a different kind of energy than what your body needs.

This is the reason I come to see you, because I know you need My nourishment for your soul, or your heart, to develop itself to its fullest potential.

Lisa: So, if I choose to turn to You, then the deepest part of my soul, as You call it, will grow. Is this correct?

God: If you observe a dog, you know that a dog will be friendly or mad according to what he perceives in front of him. If he senses you are a good person, he will be friendly, and if he senses you are not a good person, he will be mad. In a similar way, what you choose to perceive will determine which way you will grow.

Lisa: Does this mean if we choose to focus on You, our goodness and kindness will grow, and if we focus elsewhere, on someone not so good, for example, we will not grow, or even worse, grow in the opposite direction?

God: This is correct. Therefore, in order for human beings to feel there is someone good around them, I have tried for years to make them aware of and accept My existence. I have hoped that some individuals would believe in Me and recognize Me so fervently that their nature would become good enough and kind enough to be visible to those living around them. Then My hope would be that the people around these individuals could admire them and grow to become like them, instead of rejecting them.

Lisa: This makes me question, is it possible for human beings to become good if they reject You, like I used to?

God: It is possible to become good to some degree. For example, if you have a hero you can look up to, this person's goodness can create a spark in you every time you acknowledge it. This is the reason human beings are always trying to look up to someone. One reason is because they can perhaps see some part of themselves in that person, and another is because they feel something good from that person.

But the only remark I will make is, can they, through this person, receive enough elements of goodness to permit them to become as good as their potential allows?

Lisa: I remember I used to have some idols when I was younger. Today, I don't have a specific one, but I still like many different people, sometimes a writer, a singer, or an artist.

God: I believe now you understand why I want you to not forget Me, so that your internal nature can continue to develop within you to the point you can be content with yourself as a person with heart, who is kind and calm.

The place where you are now is very much a place where I remember many human beings to be. Some of them rejected

Seventh meeting

their feelings at this point. Some of them did accept to feel, but they wished to not be close to Me anymore. And some of them really comprehended that without Me, they could not be. But tragically, these ones were destroyed. This is the reason this concept of coming close to Me is so unpopular or so unknown.

But regardless of this reality, I still have to say, until you come close to the sun, you cannot feel the warmth of the sun. Until you eat a salad, the salad cannot be digested inside you. As long as you refuse to eat or drink, you will continue to be hungry and thirsty.

Lisa: I'm fascinated by Your explanation. I would never imagine it is so important to remember to be grateful to You, or to make myself aware of You in other ways.

God: It is an extremely important point that I mention to you.

Personally, I have already experienced that when a person abandoned Me or My words, for whatever reason, he first started to feel that he was empty, or in simple words, didn't feel good any more. And that person didn't just allow himself to shrivel up, like a fruit shrivels when it dries up, but he suddenly started to attack Me for not loving him, without seeing that he was the cause of not receiving love.

Lisa: So if we don't recognize You, we will turn against You?

God: Unfortunately, this will happen. The moment human beings reject the idea that I exist and no longer recognize Me or My word, their inner self will stay frozen inside of them. This coldness and the feeling of being paralyzed will make them angry towards Me, believing I am the cause of their dilemma.

It is similar to how a baby seeks food from its mother. The way it asks for food will depend on whether the baby's stomach is half full or completely empty. The more the pain of not having food inside increases, the highter the intensity of the baby's cries.

So if a human has a soul that is immensely empty, this person will have an immense tendency to become violent because of his pain, much more than the one who is maybe half full. Until human beings find the food that can make them full, they will have little choice but to be violent.

Lisa: I would never imagine Your situation to be like that. Here on Earth we try to analyze what we are going through, struggling to find some so-called solutions, but eventually we just end up trying to cover our problems.

God: I think now you understand, what I ask from your people is for their benefit, regardless it sounds like it is for Me. I do know there is a thought in the world of your people that God wants everything for Himself, and this is the reason He created human beings.

This specific thought surely did a lot of damage to human destiny, maybe not during the process of the physical lives of human beings, but surely in terms of where human beings end up after their physical body passes away. This has to be fixed sometime. My words to you, explaining that the reason I approach you is so you can receive the elements of life, will permit you to develop your inner being to the stage where you can be recognized as a being of goodness who resembles Me, or as a being of goodness who can be chosen by Me, like I wish to be chosen by you.

This is a law. Do you understand?

Seventh meeting

Lisa: Yes, My God, I do understand and I wish to have a relationship with You, not just for my benefit, but maybe also for Yours. For many years I was the person You have just described. But since the time You came to me and I became aware of Your presence with me, my happiness is at a much higher dimension than where it used to be.

God: Do you understand now that the reason I ask you to have relationship with Me is only so you can develop your goodness?

Lisa: Yes, and I hope I will not forget it, regardless I can find a million excuses. But I feel they are not important to You, and I also realize they only distract me from taking the development of my goodness seriously.

God: Yes, Lisa. Every time you accept something I say to You, especially some idea that is new to your ears, you are removing some elements of rejection from yourself. The elements that block you from believing in or from agreeing with Me are portrayed by some religious thinkers as being the cause of the death of the soul. By accepting My words, you are replacing the elements that can create death with the elements that can create life.

Lisa: What do You mean by elements of death?

God: From the very beginning of the creation of human beings, the ideal of being grateful to our parents was replaced by the situation of being angry with our parents. This has caused immense hardship for any human being who wants to choose another direction for his life, like being grateful.

Because of this reality, human beings find the struggle

between the elements of death and the elements of life as the major struggle within themselves. As well, the concept of a god of darkness against a God of light arose because of this struggle.

Until human beings win a place where they can be grateful to their parents instead of being angry with their parents, or grateful to life rather than being angry toward life, death will always rule over life.

Lisa: I have read that many religious people went to extremes because of their desire to relate with You. I had felt that they were fanatical, but now as I listen to Your explanation, I realize maybe they just felt desparate to elevate themselves in order to make a relationship with You.

God: Some time ago, people didn't have so much wealth or knowledge, yet their desire to believe in Me, to find Me and to relate with Me created a fire in them and sometimes drove them to extremes.

Tragically, it is very difficult to find the road to become one with Me, even though these people had the desire in their innermost hearts. Because they could not find peace between their inner desires and their physical desires, they often chose, as revenge, to attack the physical body that they thought was acting against their burning desire to find Me. This created even more frustration, and eventually many of them turned against Me.

Lisa: It looks like You have a lot of compassion for them, regardless I think they did hurt You.

God: Throughout My existence, My goal was to raise a model, hoping people would want to become like this model

Seventh meeting

by believing in and admiring him. But whenever a young soul decided to take the journey to become a model, it was painful to witness what could happen to him as a result, due to persecution from those around him. So I can tell you, if there were only a few who made it, there were so many more who were chosen.

Lisa: I think I am lucky to know that if I want to have a relationship with You and develop myself to become a peaceful or lovely being, what I need to do is think about You, recognize You and glorify You. I am very grateful to You for revealing to me how to grow. I also think I will not be persecuted if I try to grow, because we are living in a society where we can make our own choices.

God: Honestly speaking, because human beings have an element of rejection toward believing, trusting, and glorifying, that nature will continue to be an enemy to your choice to believe, to trust and to glorify.

So, regardless it is maybe more comfortable to be living in your present society, compared to many other times, you will still have to face, from time to time, this nature of rejection from both inside and outside you. As well, you should not judge other people for what they don't know, but you should continue to grow with what you do know, so they can eventually see what you become, because this is the only answer to what people have always tried to understand.

Lisa: You mean, even if I know the way, there will be a lot of resistance to follow it?

God: If what happens to human beings was like a fairy tale, they would be able to find Me easily, like you wanted to when you were a little girl. From time to time you chose to be good or kind to others, but sometimes you found yourself acting oppositely. The cause of this situation was provoked by the nature of destruction that was given to human beings many long years ago.

But if people can find someone in the position of parental love and learn to believe again and choose to be grateful, especially when it is not easy, they can win over the nature that wants them to choose to reject, to disbelieve or be angry at everything and everyone they live with.

Lisa: So, even if I choose to develop my internal nature, it will still not be easy.

God: Nothing is easy, because the nature of rejection basically predestines human beings to be unable to develop to the level where they can communicate with Me.

If you really want to change the pattern of this nature of rejection, you will need to practice over and over what I tell you, faster than the nature of rejection can expand itself inside you.

Lisa: I don't know exactly what You are talking about, but I think this nature must be quite powerful, because in this present time I can see the quantity of people who do not believe in You is increasing. From my own experience, too, I think this nature caused me to abandon You. Is this correct?

God: From My viewpoint, anything that stops human beings from fulfilling their destiny of goodness is a force against Me. And over time, if they accept to be governed by this force, it becomes more dominant.

But if people change their choice, then everything can be

Seventh meeting

turned around. This is the reason, throughout history, you will see human beings going from one side to another, from a place where the value of goodness becomes the tendency, to another side, where the value of matter becomes more dominant.

Lisa: So, every time I forget to think about You or to believe in You, is it because this other nature in me is also demanding my attention?

God: Yes, your perception is absolutely correct. But the real dilemma, which is maybe more dramatic than each small daily choice, is that those choices combined can create, in the long term, a very different destiny. Choosing Me will destine you to become a tree with beautiful fruits. But if you choose to believe everything is just dust, then everything existing around you will also have no great value, except to be turned into dust or ashes. This is the reason the people of your day consider that all My creation is just made to be consumed.

Lisa: So, if I choose to try to think like You, looking for the value of everything in life, will I become truly valuable?

God: Any thought that accepts and embraces life has My nature, and that thought will give you a base to receive the deepest part of My nature, which is love. This will cause your internal self to grow.

Lisa: Do You know, my God, that here we listen to lots of love songs, always dreaming about love above all else, regardless we also cry because we often don't feel love. Lots of times we end up accusing each other of not having love.

God: So, I guess I must come too late with all these theories I am telling you, because it looks like people are already singing about all the love they have. But since you tell Me they are also crying, I guess that somehow love must disappear along the way.

What is interesting about human beings is that when something is needed for their survival, a certain system within themselves starts to function and evokes the proper desire. For example, if someone does not have food, then it is the brain that will say that food needs to be eaten, based on a signal from the stomach. So if someone needs love, it is the brain that will remind them of what they need.

But what the mind of human beings can also do very well is to express their needs in different forms, like singing because they need love, or crying because they need love. In any case the reality didn't change, but because the presentation can be so drastically different, it can disturb our perception of what is really happening inside human beings.

It is easier to perceive this reality in children. For example, if a child who is hungry speaks politely when he asks for food, it is easy to assume he is not really hungry. But if a child cries or screams when he is hungry, surely you will consider he is very hungry or even starving, and therefore your reaction will be different.

So you have to look, not just at the presentation, but at the reality. Are the people who sing about love just being polite, trying to keep up the appearance of feeling the love that they don't have, and the ones who are crying just being truthful about what they don't have?

Lisa: To be honest, I think we sing about love because we don't have it. Here everyone is very sensitive about the subject of love. We are so sensitive that whenever someone says something to us, we have many ideas about that person's

Seventh meeting

motivation, about whether he says that because he loves me or because he doesn't. And at this point we often start to accuse each other.

God: Truly I can tell you, love is an element of life that transcends time and space, and circulates between every being at the speed of light. Because human beings can perceive love, they are capable of sensing when love is with them or when love is not with them.

So, whatever human beings try to believe they have, or wish to have, and so forth, they are surely not connected to My world, because when you have something in My world, you really know you have it. Therefore, there is no way you can make another interpretation. For example, when you see a stone, you cannot make an interpretation about the stone, because it exists in reality.

This is why I don't think so many philosophers of your world discuss about the nature of stones. Instead they discuss many ideas, and they don't know anything concrete about those ideas. But if they knew love was not a concept, but a reality as real as sunlight, and as solid as stones, then any discussion would disappear.

Lisa: Where does love come from? Does it come from You, or from within us, or does it exist independent from everything?

God: When you observe a tree, you can see a young tree grows from within itself and eventually becomes an adult tree. Yet the air and the sunshine that nourish it don't come from within the tree; they exist around it. Love is the same as the air and the sunshine, and you are the same as the tree. If you can receive enough love to be able to develop yourself into an adult being, then you have the potential to feel more and more love, but if you don't develop yourself, love will be unknown to you.

Lisa: Many times people here are jealous if somebody receives love. I guess it is because they didn't develop enough to receive love themselves. Then, if they perceive even a small amount of love, they are so anxious to get it, as if they were starving. This is how we live here.

God: As I said before, if human beings don't develop their goodness to the level where they can feel peace inside themselves, then no matter what they do, love will always be unknown to them. Someone who is not at peace with himself or in harmony with himself becomes like a stone wall. When love contacts that wall, it automatically bounces back to wherever it came from.

To use another example, when human beings discovered that sound waves existed, surely it was an exciting revelation for them. But the greatest discovery was when they created a receptor that was qualified to capture sound waves. Only in that moment, faster communication between human beings became available.

So, when I tell you there is love, it is like explaining there are sound waves. But if there is no receptor sensitive to that love, then love is a useless concept that you cannot comprehend until you become that receptor. Only then will you discover why I created you with so much complexity and subtlety.

Lisa: If I understand what You are trying to tell me, it is more important to grow our goodness in order to receive love than looking all around to find love. Is this correct?

God: In your world it looks like everybody is obsessed with

Seventh meeting

finding love. But I created everything based on an evolution of growth. The quality and quantity of love you can give and receive is determined by your evolution. In other words, unless human beings coordinate themselves according to the way I created things, there is no hope for them to fulfill their dreams of receiving love.

Lisa: Now I understand why You push me to follow Your guidance. It is so I can develop myself to be able to breathe the love that I dream so much about.

God: It looks like you understand everything very well. I can see you are really smart and well educated.

Lisa: I start to feel quite emotional about what You are telling me today. I'm not just learning about why we need to turn to and connect to You. I'm also realizing there were many people before me who tried to take this path, and therefore, I feel the place You want to bring me is hard to get to.

I'm feeling a little bit weak, to the point I wish to ask You if we can stop our conversation for now, because I'm overwhelmed by everything. I hope You do not feel offended and can understand my situation. As well, I hope You will come back again at another time.

God: I do understand, very well. When someone accepts to pass from knowledge to the world of feeling, that must be quite an event. It is like when someone who always flies in the clouds discovers the mechanism to pass above the clouds. Then he realizes he was not really flying before, but more like swimming, because above the clouds there is no sense of friction.

That event looks similar to passing into My world, where

only crystal clearness and vibrant colors exist. When you pass to the sphere of feeling you suddenly discover My world. And My world is many times very emotional.

So, I will depart from you now until the next time.

EIGHTH MEETING

The Rebirth of God and Lisa

This month I was very preoccupied, especially because I invited some of my friends to Thanksgiving dinner at my apartment. Preparing for this kind of event I found myself getting stretched quite thin. I worried whether my guests would come and if they would be happy with what I prepared for them. As my nervousness increased, so did my inability to be in control. Luckily there was usually no one around me to experience my outbursts.

Right before the holiday, I was so exhausted that I sat down on my couch, unable to move any more. And maybe because there was no more strength in my physical body, I started to listen to my mind and I suddenly realized someone was trying to communicate with me. I was surprised and tried to pull myself together to get ready, because I realized that Someone was my God, who after all should have the privilege to be listened to, as He was the highest of all guests for me.

Here is what my Guest had to say.

God: Lisa, are you satisfied with what you are learning and discovering? Are you happy to know that I exist?

Lisa: Yes, God, I'm very happy. But do You know, at one point in my life just the thought of Your existence bothered me?

God: I am very happy to hear you say My existence does not bother you any more, even though I do not comprehend what would bother you. If you knew what I am made of, you

Eighth meeting

would know I cannot take over your physical being or your belongings. The reality is, you do not need to make a law to prevent Me from coming, or create an army to stop Me from passing through your borders. It is much easier than that to prevent Me from visiting you.

Lisa: It was not exactly Your existence that bothered Me, but the fact that maybe I needed to think about You and Your words. I felt this would take a lot of time and effort, which I needed for other things in my life. I think it would be easy for all of us to believe in Your existence if we didn't feel we needed to do something in connection to You.

God: I am surprised to hear that, especially since you revealed yourself to Me as a person who loved the truth and was looking for your purpose in life. I cannot comprehend how it was possible your feelings could so easily command and deceive you to such a degree.

Lisa: I can only agree with You, and yet I would never have come to that awareness by myself, if You didn't come to me.

God: It looks like you are shocked to discover that reality inside yourself. But where does knowledge come from, really? Is knowledge something you create? Or is knowledge found after something is already created? Which side are you on? Are you a being who creates something, or are you someone who tries to learn about what was already created?

Interestingly, whatever side you are on, it always begins or ends with knowledge. To give an example, when someone wants to commit a crime, he has to think very ingeniously to create a plan, and after that, he commits the action. But for someone to convict him of his crime, this person has to find the

thought or the intention the criminal had, to make the conclusion it was a crime and not an accident.

Lisa: Honestly speaking, I am surprised at all the feelings I have right now. It can be really intense to meet You!

God: What are you hearing as you are feeling these emotions? What do you perceive in your head? Can you tell Me?

Lisa: I'm not sure. But I feel there is sadness inside my heart. At the same time, I hear something telling me the reason for this sadness is because I do not maintain my relationship with You.

God: Oh? It is an incredible thing that you hear! I think many people can feel sadness in themselves, but it is rare for people to connect that sadness with not having a relationship with Me. Because you can acknowledge that aspect, I will say, you are honest.

Most of the time, feelings are neglected as messages for human beings, especially when they are adults. When a young child talks to his mommy, usually he cannot explain his feelings using big philosophical concepts, therefore he just tries to say what he feels. But what is interesting, a mother always takes him seriously, regardless of his difficulty to explain his feelings.

The tragedy of being adult is, adults no longer want to listen to their feelings, and instead try to rationalize them away. If they knew feelings were the first impact of energy coming to them, or being removed from them, then they would take their feelings more seriously.

Lisa: Actually, I was surprised You asked me what I heard

Eighth meeting

when I was feeling something. Usually when we experience emotions, we just concentrate on what we feel. But You asked me to listen at the same time.

God: Let's observe the origin of feelings, in consideration that it is Me inside your heart who is happy or not happy. Surely, this thought will change the concept of what human beings are. Remember, I am omnipresent. This means I am outside as well as inside you. Therefore it is acceptable both that I am somewhere far away, and as well, I can be somewhere so close to you, to the point I am in your heart.

Based on the concept that I am in you, then when you feel happy, it is Me who is happy. And if you are not happy, it means, I am crying inside your heart.

Lisa: I cannot reason very well right now, because I'm feeling so many different emotions. But what You say must be possible.

God: If I say to you that I want you to look at yourself with the viewpoint that it is Me who is inside you, because that is the only way for you to perceive who you really are, in a pure and proper way, will you accept?

Surely this thought is not so popular in your world, regardless some philosophers have recognized that I, God, can exist in the hearts of human beings. But I do not think they perceived I was real, therefore they didn't consider their heart could be real as well.

But if they had considered I was a living identity even greater than what they already thought I was, they would surely have become so serious about what they felt in their heart, because it is through the heart I send My emotions.

The Rebirth of God and Lisa

Lisa: I must admit the concept that You can live in us is not well known to me. I have only heard that sometimes we can experience Your presence around us. In fact, some people say that we are far away from You and that You are far above us, to the point it is better not to try to talk directly to You, but instead we should try to find someone who can talk to You on our behalf.

God: Even the belief that I can be around human beings is already pretty high, considering how difficult it is for people to believe something about Me. But regardless of this belief, I have still looked for those who could accept the belief that My presence is can be within them. But you should know, in the moment someone accepts this new idea, I have the right to give him or her My feelings.

The real situation is, the beliefs of the human mind will define whether I have the right to exist and where I have the right to dwell.

Lisa: We are taught that if we believe in You, we will be able to go to heaven. What do You think about that?

God: I don't really know what your people believe, I only perceive the effect of what they believe. If they no longer want to believe in Me, I find Myself being excommunicated from this Earth. But when, for whatever reason, people reconsider believing in Me, then it is like receiving permission to be welcomed again, and eventually being able to send My presence around them.

Because they feel My love, which My presence brings, the people who allow Me to come back to this Earth feel they will be able to go to a place far better than what they experience on Earth, which is usually considered to be a place they call

Eighth meeting

heaven.

Lisa: So, do You want to say that our choice of belief affects the degree to which You can be involved in our lives?

God: I do not know what your people say when they cannot experience what I am made of, which is mainly what you call love. But from time to time, I hear people say to Me that when they feel My heart or My love, they are in heaven. It means, they really felt My presence. Nevertheless, this does not occur by accident. It occurs according to how they think.

Based on having the correct belief, they can come close to Me, which they usually consider is Me coming close to them.

Lisa: From time to time I have heard people say they felt like they were in heaven. It was a bit hard for me to understand. To me it seemed impossible to be in heaven, especially when we are here on Earth.

At other times, people have told me they experienced being in hell, describing certain events as being a nightmare. It's funny, but even though many of my friends are not religious, they still use words like heaven and hell.

God: Well, what I want to say to you now is that I can live in you, regardless it seems to be quite shocking for you to hear that, maybe because you believe you will lose your privacy, or just because you are not familiar with this idea. You might even try to scientifically analyze this event, as you often like to do. Whatever you choose to do, I still wish to ask, can you accept that I can live in you?

Before you answer, please remember what I said before. There is always an effect from a cause.

The Rebirth of God and Lisa

Lisa: I can see You allow me to choose. But it is difficult to believe that You, the almighty God who looks so big, could live in me who looks so small.

God: Yes, indeed it must be quite challenging for a young being like you to realize that I can wish to live with you or, more exactly, in you. To help you understand this concept, I can also ask, do you consider it is difficult to believe that some part of the identity of your parents is living in you? Or do you consider that you are absolutely independent from your parents?

Lisa: Of course, the fact that I have some genes or some characteristics from my parents is difficult to deny. But it makes me a little bit uncomfortable to think my parents live in me. Maybe some part of them lives in me, but I think I would prefer to believe I can create my own life and pursue my happiness without depending on my parents.

God: I do not comprehend very well what 'creating your own life' means, but I do know that you do not come from yourself alone, and you did not create yourself, did you? You must be born from someone, whom you usually call your parents, who themselves were created by your grandparents. This is the reason you are the culmination of your family line.

Regardless of what you believe, the reality is more exact than the belief.

Lisa: Does this mean that I'm destined to be just like my parents?

God: You exist because of your parents, your grandparents and many others. But the beauty of every human being is

Eighth meeting

to have the opportunity to develop and gain maturity to the point where each can look like a unique flower that everyone wishes to gaze upon and come close to. Maybe this is what, in your language, you call 'trying to find yourself' or 'finding your identity'.

Lisa: I feel I need to say sorry to You. Because of Your explanation, which I cannot dispute, I realize that I tend to live alone and deny my roots, my parents. However, in general I do appreciate and love them.

God: Oh, I am surprised to see you becoming humble in front of Me. This is rare to see on your part, maybe because I am not convincing enough for you. Therefore, something big must have happened for you to be sorry, hasn't it?

Lisa: Honestly speaking, My God, it's because what You say to me is so convincing that I feel sorry. I'm used to people talking to me, but usually I don't listen so carefully to them, because the contents of their talk is mainly filled with things I already know or can predict. But when I listen to You, I cannot predict at all what You will say. I'm surprised over and over. This is the reason I'm so attracted, and so sorry, based on all the wrong thoughts I used to have.

God: There is an expression I have heard many times, that light can remove darkness. Therefore, the only hope for human beings is to find a new concept of knowledge that has more light than the former one. If this happens, surely people will feel shocked to see everything they used to know or believe change when that new light comes.

So, I believe for you to be able to say 'sorry', it must mean that My knowledge is bringing more brightness to the place

where your being dwells, and this new brightness is enabling you to see that your former knowledge had less light than what I bring to you now.

Lisa: Yes, it does feel brighter as I try to accept Your viewpoint that You can live in my heart, regardless I do not perceive so well what this can mean.

God: A long time ago, when the human race was in the process of being formed, I made them in a way they could have the ability to relate with Me, because that would please Me. In order for them to be able to achieve that relationship, I planted a seed inside them, and from that seed, they could mature themselves to the level where their character could resemble My goodness.

Lisa: Do you know, my God, this idea will be challenging for people to accept, because we are raised with the concept that everything that cannot be proven, cannot be true, regardless You explain how it can be possible.

God: Your education is impressive to Me. It seems to be quite systematic and organized. As you said, something must be logical in order for you to be able to recognize it as being true.

But besides that, I want to tell you, if you discover a part of yourself that doesn't yet seem to be logical, it does not mean it is not true, but instead it is in the stage of being unknown. If you accept to go inside this unknown area, after a while you will realize this unknown characteristic also contains logic, and this will permit you to relate to it and add it to what you already understand. Then, you will be able to make the conclusion that it is true.

Eighth meeting

Lisa: Your words confront me, because even though I see myself as an adventurous person, I realize I like to go to places where it's somehow secure and I can to some degree predict what will happen. It's challenging for me to think about exploring an unknown or unpopular area or concept.

God: I do agree with you, Lisa, that it must be challenging to believe it can be true that I, the Creator of the Universe, who lives somewhere in the sky, can have a connection with a miniscule being like you. On the other hand, if that potential were not there, you would never have questioned the possibility of having a relationship with Me in the first place, because it is impossible to question something that does not have the capacity to be true.

Lisa: Yes, indeed. I remember when I was younger, the question of whether I could talk to You came to my mind sometimes. But I didn't feel I could mention it to my friends or to my parents. So, I kept this question to myself and tried to bury it.

God: If you want to know, every thought originates from some form of matter or energy, created by the laws of physics or metaphysics. The moment there is an aspect of identity, a thought is created and emerges. Then it is possible for any human being who is honest and sensitive to realize there is an origin connected to that thought in the realm of physics or metaphysics somewhere.

This is the reason the idea that I exist is not just coming to you today, but has carried on through all the ages of human history. Not because people knew yet who I was, but because they just sensed I was. Based on that, they started to create resemblances of Me, or find symbols that could be used as

representations of Me.

Regardless of these events, there was some rage from time to time passing over the planet Earth, like a dark cloud, which came to try to remove all these symbols that people believed in.

But after this madness passed, people rebuilt their resemblances or their edifices, or whatever symbolized the force of goodness that was bigger than themselves, which they sensed existed somewhere.

Lisa: I believe You want to tell me this so I can realize that if I had questions about You, it was because of the reality of Your existence somewhere.

God: To answer your statement I will simply say 'yes'. This theory that every thought is connected to an origin doesn't only work concerning your perception of Me, but also applies when you sense things around you that are not yet understood, but exist in the stage of perception.

Then, from these perceptions, human beings begin to research the things that exist around them. When someone first saw a mushroom, for example, something told him that it was maybe edible. But only after testing the mushroom would human beings absolutely know. However at first, it was their thoughts that gave them some perceptions about what was around them.

The reason human beings could begin to find knowledge was because they began to submit to their perceptions. From that stage, they could easily go to the field of finding the mechanisms that were involved.

So, if human beings today accept to recognize what they perceive about Me, they will also be able to develop the knowledge that goes with it, and from that, they will discover what I am made of, and who they are.

Eighth meeting

Lisa: When I am relaxing over the weekend, I sometimes think about how it will be on Monday morning when I return to my office, and I have different kinds of thoughts and emotions. Sometimes I feel happy, and other times I feel a little bit nervous and wish I wouldn't have to go in.

Would you consider I am perceiving thoughts coming from the realm of my workplace?

God: I am pleased by the way you learn things so fast. I think your example is a good one. You did not make any mistake in perception based on what I taught you.

Lisa: So, if it's true that I perceive thoughts from different realms, the question is, should I be concerned about what I hear or is it better not to pay much attention?

God: If you develop the quality of being able to perceive thoughts coming from different realms of existence, you can learn many things according to how much you can believe in your perceptions. If you reject believing in the thoughts from your perceptions, they will not have any meaning for you, but this will not change the reality of the vibrations your office emits, because these vibrations did not disappear. It is just that you erased what you perceived and heard.

Lisa: So, if I do not want to believe in something, I am just denying an existing reality but not removing it?

God: Exactly. Can you be more aware now that the effect of not believing in something is to make you deny the reality of that thing?

So, for a person who believes visible matter is the only source of reality, and that nothing else should be perceived

nor any thought should be connected to it, it must be a shock to realize that thoughts can be created or perceptions received from various sources of reality, don't you think?

Lisa: Yes, I am a bit shocked. Do you know, My God, I claim to be a realistic person, logical and down to earth, only considering scientific facts as legitimate truths. But now I realize if I am not receptive to a thought I receive, I might reject a physical or a metaphysical reality at the same time.

God: So, after My explanation, can you believe that My existence can be living inside of you? What are you going to perceive?

Lisa: Yes, I can now believe this thought must come from some kind of possible reality, even though I'm not yet familiar with the realm of metaphysics You speak about. Since the idea that You can live in me exists, it means there must be some reality connected to it.

God: The moment you decide to believe in or to submit to this view that I can exist inside your heart, in that moment you are actually initiating the process of creating the seed of My existence in you. Then it is understandable that the seed of Me in you will soon demand to develop itself into an adult being, who can fully satisfy the Me who is also the Almighty God.

Lisa: If I accept the idea that there is a seed of You inside me looking for You, the God of the Universe, does this mean I will always need to act according to the wishes of that seed?

God: I do not know what you should do, as I also do not

Eighth meeting

know what it is like to live in opposition to the wish of the most profound part of yourself.

Lisa: You know, God, before I heard Your voice coming to me, it was easy to live just how I wished. But from the time I started to hear You, I realized I needed to restrain some of my activities, especially connected to what I think and what I talk about. And now, after You introduce the reality of Your seed inside me, it looks like again, one more time, I have to reconsider what I am doing, based on keeping this seed alive and growing.

It seems it was easier to live before, because I didn't need to worry about the concept of You in me.

God: I guess that time must have been very peaceful since you did not hear so many different voices inside you, besides the ones you considered necessary to follow for your livelihood.

Since you like to visit parks, have you noticed that there are some parks where trees grow without anyone pruning them, and there are other parks where humans are constantly behind the scenes, cleaning up branches and directing the trees toward certain shapes? Regardless everything can be considered beautiful, to which park are human beings more attracted? And also, which park has a more difficult life, compared to the other one?

Lisa: Well, I don't think human beings want to know that in order to become beautiful they need to go through some 'pruning'. Therefore, our first tendency would be to choose the park that does whatever it likes. But the reality is, we will just pass quickly through this park, but will take time to admire the other one, bringing our friends and our cameras with us.

The Rebirth of God and Lisa

God: So indeed, a park that accepts to go through hardships can have the pleasure of being visited more often. It is similar with human beings.

One of the reasons human beings have difficulty accepting thoughts from Me is because they always want to frame each thought within the known laws of physics. When a thought does not fit in, usually because that thought is bigger than the frame itself, then human beings have a tendency to reject it, fearing the difficulty of expanding their frame to fit this new thought.

This event often occurs in younger beings. Because their molecules are so tight and their energy is so high, they don't easily believe in anything I present to them.

But by the time a human being gets a little bit older, like you now, the molecular mechanisms start to become a bit slower and more transparent, in other words, less solid. This allows human beings to be more capable of perceiving metaphysical thoughts. Therefore, the more human beings age, the more easily they can acknowledge or accept such a thought as Me existing inside them, compared to when they were younger.

Lisa: Hmm, that's very interesting.

God: So, to bring you back to My previous view, when I said to you that My seed is inside you, what further preoccupies Me is the question of whether this seed will die with you after your flesh has consummated its time, or whether it will have a chance to develop itself fully through the process of your physical time of existence.

Lisa: I start to perceive Your concern is not only whether we believe You exist in us or not, but whether or not Your seed

Eighth meeting

can develop itself to its full potential.

God: Of course, I think it is a major victory for human beings to acknowledge that I can live in them. But they need to also acknowledge that if a land cannot nourish its seeds, that land feels useless and doesn't mind drying up or dying. On the other hand, if a land accepts its responsibility and fulfills its destiny to nourish the seeds planted in it, I think this land will feel immense pleasure and purpose to exist.

Lisa: According to what You're saying, it looks like You imply that our flesh is like a plot of land, and if our flesh does not acknowledge and nourish Your seed, then it feels useless and depressed, because it has no purpose.

God: I have heard that on your planet many individual people or groups of people do not consider the physical life as being so valuable. This is because they did not yet arrive to the level where they could believe that I could live in them. Because of this incapacity to recognize My seed inside them, they feel the value of the flesh is insignificant.
 Therefore, human beings throughout history have often used their flesh in an extreme way, destroying themselves and others at the same time.

Lisa: Based on what You tell me, I can now see the value of my physical body. But I don't think I would have been able to discover Your viewpoint about this on my own. I thought the situation You have just described was sad but accepted it as a normal part of our world.

God: So, Lisa, do you now believe that you have My seed in you and that during your physical existence you have the

The Rebirth of God and Lisa

responsibility to nurture that seed?

Lisa: Yes, My God, I do accept Your explanation. At the same time lots of questions are coming to my mind. For example, how do we develop the nature that comes from You? And why is it our responsibility to take care of this nature that belongs to You?

God: If you look beyond your planet or listen to your scientists who observe other planets, you will hear their voices as well as your own asking, "Do other planets have life on them?" In other words, you want to know whether there are other planets where the seeds of trees and flowers can grow.

So, when you ask Me why you need to be responsible to mature My seed in you, I think it is because you do not know the misery of being a planet where nothing can grow.

Lisa: Well, it's just that I hadn't heard the concept of developing You from within myself. Religious people only tell us that if we have faith in You, we will be saved.

God: If you give birth to a baby, should you as the mother be responsible to give nourishment to the baby, or should the baby, who does not know yet who it is or what it needs, go shopping and cook food for itself? Your motherly instinct surely will answer to Me, "Of course not."

So, the first step in maintaining the survival of your seed is to learn to be aware of it before you are aware of yourself. This is the first difficulty you will face. When you start to be more aware of your seed, then you will start to discover your natural instinct is to try to nourish this seed. Then, through how well you take care of it, you will know how good a mother you are.

Eighth meeting

Lisa: I can now see that I'm responsible to grow the seed that is living in me, like a mother who protects and feeds her child.

God: Yes, Lisa, you are responsible to give nourishment to the seed within you, which is a most miniature part of Me planted in you at the present stage of your existence.

Lisa: But I feel You didn't answer my question about those religious thinkers who claim we can be saved by having faith in You.

God: Have patience. Answers are not just words that we arrange to sound good; answers must make sense. They must be able to explain something. Lisa, I have explained many things to you to help you believe in Me, which is the beginning of all beginnings. By explaining about My presence in you, I hope you can eventually turn to Me everyday and in that way receive the life element to nourish the seed living in you, which you are just beginning to discover.

If your religious thinkers or teachers had turned to Me more often, perhaps as often as the hands of a clock arrive to every hour or even to every minute, they would already have discovered that they were not just meant to be believers in salvation, but beings whom I could call My sons and My daughters.

Lisa: Your answer does not seem to completely reject what they teach, but at the same time it looks like they didn't achieve Your dream, did they?

God: If you have some land and you plant flowers in it, will you be more concerned about how much you believe in the

seeds, or whether the seeds develop? The tragedy of human beings is they do not have knowledge about how they grow, regardless they have immense knowledge about the physical universe. They still question the meaning and purpose of their existence, and so many other questions, I guess. They look like they are in the middle of something they do not know anything about.

Unless human beings accept to learn who they are and what they need to do to grow, they cannot begin to create what they are meant to be.

Lisa: Of course, I want Your seed to sprout and bloom in me, because I now understand who I am, and the purpose of my physical being.

God: So, do you understand now why I have been trying to teach you how to look at life and how to perceive yourself? This has been for the single purpose of creating the best conditions for you to come to believe I can live in you. From there, you can receive My love, which is needed for the nourishment of My seed in you.

Lisa: Yes, You've explained to me about how to create a peaceful mind in order to help me to listen to my conscience, and about inviting You instead of demanding that You come, about valuing each part of myself, and so many other things. I see now that this was all in order for me to understand that I need to receive Your love so I can grow Your seed in me.

God: I think from this moment on, there will be no more questions coming from you concerning My existence. You will no longer believe I am far away in the sky, at a seemingly endless distance, when you call for Me. From now on, you

Eighth meeting

will find that you can easily say that I am with you and I am accompanying you everywhere you go.

This, Lisa, can be possible because you accept today that I am inside of you.

Lisa: I feel so happy to know that. At the same time I feel anxious about my responsibility to make You grow within me.

God: Yes, Lisa, I dearly wish and expect that you will make a great deal of effort so My little seed does not stay dormant, but instead can become an adult one day. When that seed arrives to adulthood, I will be able to recognize your qualification as a mature being who resembles Me.

Lisa: My God, I want to say to You that I promise to carry Your seed in me and I feel responsible to nurture it, regardless I know it won't be easy.

God: The moment you comprehend that My seed is in you, you will realize it is actually like carrying an embryo or a fetus. In that sense it is like you are pregnant and, from this moment, you are responsible to make sure the fetus does not die, by nourishing it with love, which I am responsible to give to you.

So, go in peace.

Lisa: I want to say thank you, my God, and I'll try to do my very best!

Notes from Lisa

After God left I continued to write in my journal, because I wanted to express how amazing this meeting was for me. First of all, what God told me was unknown to me before. At the same time, I experienced many new feelings. In this meeting I felt God's touch was like velvet, and made me feel tender.

I have tried to explain everything in detail so you, too, can in some way experience this same emotion while reading my journal. As well, I felt I needed to quickly write down all that happened to me before I became distracted by other events of life.

NINTH MEETING

The Rebirth of God and Lisa

The holiday season was so full that I became completely preoccupied with many small details. But as the holidays started to fade from my memory, I began to feel settled again and my mind returned to our last meeting. I became more sensitive to the different feelings within me, knowing they were God's feelings in me. I became aware of a deep longing to meet God again. I dearly hoped He would have some time to come to visit me.

Then one weekend, as I was looking around my apartment, I got an idea to redecorate it, to make it more colorful by adding some stencils. I just felt I needed to change something and after I did, I felt pleased at the effect.

I was eager to share my enthusiasm wtih God, and one evening He came again.

God: I have come to visit you today. Are you pleased about that or were you already fully content?

Lisa: I was longing for You to come! I can feel so much happiness inside of me to be, I'm not sure how to say it, in front of You, or at Your side, or to the left or right of You.

God: I can see it is not easy to express your feeling in words, especially when the feeling is all around you. Your explanation proves that My presence manifests itself through a spherical and not through a frontal system, doesn't it?

Ninth meeting

Lisa: Yes, that's it exactly! Through Your answers I can always perceive things better. But I begin to understand why a person who has met You has immense difficulty to explain what he or she feels. I remember, I once met someone who had an experience with You, but this person had such a hard time explaining that I rejected her experience, saying it could not be true.

But now, I think I understand her difficulty and her frustration a little bit, because I also feel it is so difficult to explain about You, even though I have a pretty good vocabulary.

God: I am very pleased to know the effect I have in you. Always remember, as long as you respond by trying to express your understanding or your feelings to Me, I will feel welcome to visit you.

There is one thing you may have noticed about human beings. If you ask them what they feel, they often respond that they cannot explain or it is not easy to put into words. It looks similar when someone tries to figure out what I am. No one can explain who I am, and I know that. Therefore, because I know so well about this difficulty, I created physical things for people to use to help them describe Me.

But I have also heard, if someone tries to explain his or her experience through examples from physical matter, others don't consider it can be Me. Therefore, this dilemma continues to be a major obstacle in explaining who or what I am, as well as what you feel.

So, besides that, did you say to Me you are happy that I came? Then the question is, who is happy? Is it you yourself who is happy or is it the seed inside of you, which is actually your future self, who is happy?

Lisa: Oh, You remember very well what You said to me last time! Do You know, Your words challenged me to the point that sometimes I just wanted to put them away in a secret place deep inside of me? But at other times, I felt like shouting Your words to the world. And today, You come back to the exact same point.

God: How can I forget reality? I can forget words but not reality. The reality brings back the words to Me.

So, if you are happy, will you consider you together with Me as happy, or does your happiness have a separate identity from Me?

Lisa: In the past, I felt my happiness was created only by me. However, I now know Your happiness and mine are intertwined.

God: Yes, only if you identify your happiness as also My happiness, will you be able to consider you and I are one and realize that I can experience the feelings inside you. Then, you will be able to experience My feelings inside you.

Lisa: You have made me realize that my feelings are actually a combination of You and me, but I still have one question. Is there anything that belongs to me?

God: The 'you' alone is like a piece of land, in other words, your physical existence. The innermost part of you, your 'self', is Me and you. When you say you are happy, that happiness comes from the inner part of yourself, the 'Me and you'.

I heard, in your world, people always want to make sure they are separate or distinct from others. But do you consider a positively charged particle can separate itself from a negatively charged particle and still create something? Or is

Ninth meeting

it because the two become one, that they can become an atom?

Surely in My sight, two becoming one always creates something with more beauty and strength than two individuals separate from each other, who appear to Me to be vulnerable and endangered.

Lisa: So, my God, this means whenever I don't feel happy, it's a sign that You are not happy?

God: This is absolutely right, based on the dimension I explain now. If you are sensitive and sincere with yourself and if you care about your feelings, you will realize the Me in you, which is like a fetus growing inside you, is many times demanding food. When this fetus receives food, then you can perceive its happiness.

Therefore, when you say you are happy to see Me, it is your fetus who is happy, knowing that it will receive nourishment from Me.

Lisa: Within the last few weeks I felt from time to time that I needed something, which I believed to be some kind of spiritual nourishment, as it is called by religious people here. But without Your explanation I would never have realized that this feeling of lack of nourishment is actually because of Your fetus living in me.

God: I have heard your religious thinkers preaching many times that human beings need spiritual food. Yet I never understood their explanation of the purpose of that nourishment. It is not meant just so you can be called to go to heaven, or to help you maintain your desire to support what they call 'the church's mission'. It is meant to nourish the fetus in you, who will become your true 'self', and with whom I can relate fully, according to who I am.

The moment you and your people accept the way you are created, it will be easy for you to understand the concept that only nourishment fitting to the fetus can make you, or your fetus, feel happy.

In other words, if you give the wrong nourishment to your fetus, you cannot be happy. If everybody understood that, how simple human existence would be, and how easily human beings would become what they were originally planned to be!

Lisa: Many times, when I experienced sadness, I tried to lessen this feeling by calling a friend, going shopping or using other tactics. And I did feel some temporary release from my unhappiness.

But according to what I understand now, I question whether I did the right thing, if I consider it was Your fetus in me who was demanding food.

God: Many of your people behave exactly the way you do. They use techniques like going shopping, watching a movie and so forth. This is the reason I seldom see people coming to Me to receive the elements that can truly satisfy them. If they came, I would know them and they would know Me.

But I do believe, today, no one knows Me, because they never came to Me. Therefore, there must be a lot of your people who have an immense need of nourishment, don't you think?

Lisa: When I hear You saying that about other people, I'm a little bit surprised. I did consider that some of my religious acquaintances were somehow communicating with You through their prayers and services.

God: It is possible that your friends perform rituals or pray

Ninth meeting

with the thought to please Me or to communicate with Me. But the point is, are they receiving the nourishment they need from Me to develop their inner being, or fetus? If not, then if they are sincere they will know they are malnourished, because they will still feel unsatisfied.

But regardless they are not satisfied, do they try to find another way of receiving nourishment from Me? Or are they content to stay with their fate?

Lisa: Through what You're saying, I realize to be a believer does not guarantee we have a relationship with You. Faith doesn't automatically allow us to receive nourishment for ourselves. Is this true?

God: Let Me explain. A person who believes in something is usually a person who acknowledges that something does exist. But many believers don't try to relate with that Existence, which is Me, therefore their belief becomes something static and not something that transmits energy. That belief causes them to be neutral and to not to try to reciprocate.

If I am asked to recognize the value of believing, I will indeed agree that a believer does something good. But that doesn't necessarily mean this person has discovered how to move in My direction. Many believers still demonstrate the need to find nourishment, because they don't have a connection with Me.

Lisa: Oh, I think I understand now why people can believe it is somehow arrogant to have the desire to be in relationship with You. Maybe this viewpoint came because people could not achieve a relationship with You, and this is why they rejected the idea.

God: It is very interesting, even surprising, for Me to hear the concept that if someone dared to want some kind of relationship with Me, this person would become arrogant. As a matter of fact, the most difficult thing to do is to create a relationship with Me, or to receive elements from My deepest part, since it requires a person to be absolutely humble and sincere.

Therefore, I cannot understand why human beings who try to find Me would be called arrogant.

Lisa: I don't know the origin of that statement. But from my own experience, when I saw someone who believed in You and tried to talk to You, I also realized that person had a certain confidence. I think this confidence is what bothers people, therefore to purposely hurt this person they will say to him that he is arrogant.

God: Oh, I see. Then, if someone claims to have a relationship with Me, this must be the supremacy of arrogance. How about if someone nourishes the fetus inside of himself to the point the fetus becomes mature, what will you call this person, the devil?

Lisa: After following Your logic, it doesn't make sense to label someone who wants to relate with You as being arrogant. I can see it is actually more like an act of arrogance if we reject this possibility.

Therefore, I want to apologize to You for being that kind of person for so many years before You came to visit me.

God: Any moment You try to turn to Me, to more deeply believe in My existence or to want to have a relationship with Me, those events already demand humility from you.

Ninth meeting

That humility plus My nature coming into you through that passageway will not weaken you or make you vulnerable, but instead will give you a higher level of confidence.

Lisa: Does this mean every time I try to turn to You or follow what You tell me, I need to start with humility?

God: Every time I give you another level of understanding, you need to make a new effort of humility to receive it. But if My words are the same words as were given centuries ago, you would not expand your quantity of humility and you would stagnate.

Yes, indeed, humility is an immensely important requirement for being able to approach Me and even more so for having a relationship with Me.

Lisa: So now, after finding myself wanting more and more to have a relationship with You, where do I go from here?

God: In the moment you view yourself as being the womb for your fetus or the land for the seed in you, or the mother for your child, you will be deeply concerned about making sure this new identity can have a chance to develop and to mature itself.

Lisa: My God, do You really think I can see myself as a mother?

God: Yes, I do. I created human beings' bodies in such a way that they could be transparent enough for My energy to pass through them to nourish My fetus. But at the same time, human beings are made in a way that My nourishment can only become available to them through their system of thought or consciousess, which permits them to receive energy from

Me for My fetus in them, nourishing it to maturity. At that point, they would become one with My identity.

If you want to make sure My fetus, which will become your future mature self, can receive the elements of life, I will ask you to consciously identify the feelings coming from your innermost part as being the fetus' expressions. I hope you will follow its demands, because this fetus will tell you whether or not you have properly carried out your responsibility to nurture it.

Lisa: Then if I do not feel happy, I need to find the nourishment that can remove my feeling of unhappiness, until I can feel happy again?

God: Yes. For example, if a mother sees her child crying for food, her instinct demands her to look for food fitting to her child, until her child feels content again. Therefore, if you really care for your fetus or your future self, you will take the role of a mother to it for some period of time. In this position of mother, you will look for the right kind of nourishment until your fetus has matured to a point where it can receive its nourishment directly.

Lisa: I feel worried about whether I can take this task seriously enough.

God: I think you are anxious because you take very seriously that you are carrying Me in you, to the point you do not want to make Me, or your fetus, suffer. Instead, it seems you want to learn to nourish your fetus so that your future self can have love, isn't that true?

Lisa: Yes, that's true. You are the Creator of my soul and You

Ninth meeting

are the God who is Omnipresent.

God: Those are sophisticated words, but I do not consider Myself to be quite what you say I am, based on what I have been describing to you today.

Lisa: Oh, then, what do You consider Yourself?

God: I am a parent who hopes that a young child can develop herself and be transformed into an adult being who can be called My daughter.

TENTH MEETING

Tenth meeting

Many times I took the opportunity to reread God's words. I was sometimes surprised to see the way I responded to God. I realized that my answers did not always correspond to what He asked me, even though at the time I was sincere in replying to Him. It surprised me to see that, because I thought of myself as a logical person, especially since in my job I expected others to respond clearly to the questions I asked of them.

While reading all these questions and answers, I was amazed by the way God never lost His track but instead maintained His idea regardless of how confusing my responses were. He kept focused on what He wanted to say, even though I responded to Him based on various thoughts coming to my head from what I had heard somewhere or somehow believed to be true. He didn't seem to be affected, and perhaps was even amused sometimes by my responses, I'm not sure. Overall I was shocked to find that two different beings, God and I, with maybe very little in common, could share something with each other.

I hope you, too, feel interested in reading what God has to say, regardless it is not always easy to comprehend or to accept. Yet I think, on the whole, His words are so powerful that they can make us want to change our lives. To begin with, I have immensely changed the views I had from my previous education, or wherever they came from. I have found myself rejecting some things I used to like, as well as welcoming some things I used to dislike. It is possible that you, too, will find some changes in your views, and I deeply hope you are not afraid to welcome these changes.

After a couple of months passed, God came to visit me again. At that time I was in the process of preparing for a conference. I was rushing around, but knowing that God comes so rarely and feeling that I would be very sad if I didn't welcome Him, I stopped everything I was doing to listen to Him. I was determined to welcome whatever He would tell me.

 The Rebirth of God and Lisa

God: Hello! Is someone there?

Lisa: Yes, yes, I'm here! I'm sorry, I've been a bit preoccupied.

God: Do you think I am coming too often to you? Do you think maybe I am talking too much to you?

Lisa: Well, it does look like You have a lot of things to tell me. Maybe it's because You have so much to say, or maybe You don't have a lot of chances to say what You want to say, I'm not sure.

God: So, Lisa, can I continue from our last meeting? Do you remember what I talked to you about the last time?

Lisa: Yes, I do remember what You taught me. I would think it might be difficult for You to remember what You said to me, because You must have visited many people since the time You last talked to me.

God: For you to make this remark concerning Me, you must have some experience of talking to people and therefore know how difficult it is to always remember what you said to them.
 One thing is sure, though, knowledge is like food. When you are at a certain level in your process of evolution, I know what food, or what knowledge, you need to have at that level, and that gives Me an absoluteness of memory. From there, I know what you need in order to continue your journey.

Lisa: Yes, I do speak to many people, and my major challenge is to make sure I don't repeat the same thing to the same person, because then that person might think I don't care about him or her.

Tenth meeting

God: It must be very tough to live on your planet. How is it possible that you might not please somebody just because you repeat the same thing to him, or because you don't remember what you talked about before?

Lisa: It's not easy here. People are often extremely sensitive. A little something can cause them to turn their back on you, or stop talking to you. So many times, we need to apologize to someone.

God: I thought you only dealt with management. I didn't realize you also deal with the nature of human beings.

Lisa: Well, part of management means dealing with people's emotions. Some people aren't afraid to show me when they are displeased because I do not perceive their moods, which are always changing. I need to learn to act, to some degree, according to what others expect from me. Many emotions can arise at our meetings, to the point we can easily forget what we came for in the first place, which was for business.

God: So, if you deal with people, similar as I do, would it not be preferable for you to always remember that I am living inside of you, because this could help you to find the best wisdom to deal with each person in the most lovely way?

Lisa: Yes, from the viewpoint of expertise, I'm sure You are much more aware than I of what human beings are about. Therefore, I think it would be wise for me to learn from You how to deal with people.

God: Since I am more expert in this field than you, the only way for Me to help you is to co-exist with you, in other words,

to be able to be alive inside of you.

But am I sleeping or awake inside of you during many moments? Do you live with the awareness of Me being inside of you, or do you just fulfill your daily routine of life without realizing I am in you?

Lisa: I have to admit many times I'm busy with my life and I forget You are inside of me. But I want to gain this awareness.

God: Do you know, the human mind has many capabilities? One is the ability to have something written upon it, another is the ability to have knowledge removed.

I don't know whether you are aware that your mind has this potential to be written upon, or to be erased, with a special kind of pencil and eraser. I consider this is something fantastic that I created inside the mind of human beings.

Lisa: Yes, I can perceive somthing like that inside me.

God: Every time I meet you, I am trying to write something new in you. Today I am trying to write that I want to be alive inside of you.

But before you can experience this as a reality, you can question it, believing it or not believing it. If you decide to believe it, then it will be written inside of you and will stay written inside of you. If you decide not to believe it, this idea will be erased from inside of you, to the point you will not remember it.

Therefore, the special eraser is to not believe, and the special pencil is to believe. Would you agree with that?

Lisa: Your explanation is very impressive, my God. Many times I saw people question whether or not to believe in

Tenth meeting

something. But I couldn't imagine the effect that beliefs have on our brain or on our knowledge in general.

God: The most difficult thing for Me has been to find someone who accepts to believe in something and then to never erase it, or to erase it only when I bring a new thought for him or her to believe in. I expect and wish that person could at least maintain belief in My word for a certain period of time without introducing other words or replacing My words.

Then, I would consider this person to be very gentle with his or her soul.

Lisa: So, My God, if I choose Your viewpoint that You are living in me and believe in it, this belief will eventually become a reality?

God: Yes, the reality of an idea can only be perceived when it is fulfilled in substance. To give an example to you, when someone wants to create a pond, he needs to first believe in the idea of creating a pond. Then he needs to make a hole in the ground. Finally, when the water enters, the reality of his idea is achieved; it becomes substance.

So, if you believe that I am in you, it is similar to believing in the idea of creating a pond. If you live according your belief, it is like you are creating a basin inside your land. Then My love can go inside you and fill you up, and you will perceive the substance of your belief because I will have become the substantial God in you.

From that moment, you will no longer be capable of not believing. Can you understand now?

Lisa: Yes. From Your explanation I can perceive why You say it is not easy for You to find someone who can maintain his

or her belief. I remember there were times in my life when nothing seemed sure. Maybe that was because I didn't yet believe in anything.

God: By the way you answer Me, I can see the effect My teaching has in you. I am pleased you are trying to understand Me.

Lisa: And I'm very happy that You say that!

God: So, can you now accept that the Me who is living inside of you has desires? Do you believe I should just be dormant or sleeping inside of you, or should you respond to Me according to My desire to develop inside of you? By responding you allow the Me inside of you to grow, which will result in a wonderful feeling as well as a sense of accomplishment during your long eternal life.

Lisa: So, through believing that You are in me and trying to respond to Your desires, are You saying that I can nourish and develop the You in me to the point where I will feel I have achieved something great in my life?

God: When someone can become a substantial Me, I will not be content to call this person My 'achievement', but instead I will call you My 'daughter', because you were so faithful and loyal to allow the Me inside of you to exist, to begin with, and also to care for My development.

Lisa: Do You want to tell me that I can actually be Your daughter and therefore I can consider You to be my Father?

God: If I look at you today, I cannot yet say to you that you

Tenth meeting

are My daughter in substance. But because you accept to believe I am living in you and you do not erase this idea, you are showing a deep interest in becoming My daughter.

Lisa: I think right now I need some air! It's not because what You say is difficult to comprehend, but because my emotions start to overflow. I was not really prepared for this.

God: You feel a lot of emotion? Indeed, I can really believe that you are changing! It is quite a transformation to see you becoming such an emotional being in front of Me, instead of just a rational being who only understands things based on logic.

Let Me explain one thing. The more an object is compact, the less air can pass through it, and because of this it can maintain itself longer. However, it becomes as hard as stone. On the other hand, when things allow more air to pass within them, they will perhaps not be as durable, but they will become soft and tender, like fruits, to the point you will want to eat them.

It seems like your structure of logic is no longer as tight as it was and because of that, a lot of air can pass through you. Now, can you describe your emotions to Me?

Lisa: I'm not sure what this emotion is, but it's like a current of electricity pulsing through me, creating a vibration every time it passes. Can You understand this explanation?

God: I do understand the system of electricity very, very well, because it was My major. I think you were smart to choose this explanation.

Every vibration brings movement, and every movement brings a sort of friction. Finally, when the 'friction' becomes

strong, it provokes emotion in the system of human beings. In the realm of the universe, you can call it electricity.

Lisa: I'm really surprised I have become so emotional about the idea that I can be Your daughter. Does it mean there is some movement inside myself that is creating friction?

God: Yes, in the moment you grow and develop the Me inside of you, you are going to perceive a new level of relationship or vibration with Me. And, if you are persistent in maturing the Me in you, as My daughter, then at a certain point you will discover that nothing can separate or divide the divine you from your Father.

Lisa: Usually when people discuss about where You live, the conversation can become quite heated. It seems we have to be very careful about what we say, and our explanations are quite vague. But You definitely know what You are talking about, since You speak so clearly and directly about this subject.

God: If you mature your 'self' who carries the Me in you to the level where I as the Father can relate with you as the daughter, then indeed, whatever joy I have can at the same moment be perceived by you as your joy.

And, concerning this dimension, I can tell you that no physical concept or theory can fully explain this reality.

Lisa: That sounds wonderful! Regardless I haven't yet experienced this event, something tells me this is the way it should be. Maybe my intuition tells me, or maybe it's my mind, I don't know. Yet, what You say seems so normal, as if it were already written in me.

Tenth meeting

God: You are correct. We are made to be One. The moment you realize you carry My fetus inside of you and you take responsibility to grow it by making a relationship with the Me outside of you, we start to revolve around each other to the point where we become One, as I originally planned for human beings. And from this Oneness with Me, you can become one with any other human being who fulfills the same achievement.

Lisa: After passing through all these emotions, I think I need to come back to the beginning of Your lesson to me, which is to keep the belief that You want to be alive and awake inside of me.

God: Yes, if you can maintain that belief, you are no longer alone, and I can come to visit you whenever I wish. But the moment you lose or erase this belief, I can no longer see nor find you, and I will be unable to come back to you until you re-find that truth and believe in it again.
Are you going to avoid this tragic situation?

Lisa: Yes, I think I understand now why it's necessary for me to not just allow You to be dormant inside me but to keep an awareness of You in order for You to be fully awake inside of me.

God: I have heard there are many human beings created in physical matter, but from My point of view they are not yet created as long as they erase the idea that I am a part of their life, as much as their eyes are a part of their face.
In order for Me to perceive human beings as My embodiments, they need to have the same nature and the same heart as I have. Until then, I will not and I cannot perceive

them as beings created in My image.

Only when human beings accept the reality that I am meant to exist in them and they respond to this reality with honor and loyalty, in that moment can I start to manifest some part of Myself in them. And eventually, over time, I will see the substantial result in them to the point I can freely relate with them as mature beings.

Lisa: Now I can see, God, a little bit from Your viewpoint. I really understand that our having a physical body is not of major importance for You, but rather, whether we recognize Your existence in us as well as develop the You in us.

God: Yes, now you understand My viewpoint very well. Remember forever, I cannot change this fact because I am a God of love and I can only relate with someone who also has mature love.

As you may know, what is created according to certain laws can only function through those laws. And to function through those laws, it has to follow them.

Lisa: But do You know, I'm still afraid that finding food for Your fetus in me will become a major challenge, because here on Earth we are all so preoccupied with our daily lives. We use a lot of time to learn all kinds of things and to accomplish many different physical tasks.

This is why I believe it won't be easy for me to remember to nourish myself, or in other words, to nourish the You in me.

God: I have heard this explanation from many people I have met during My time of existence. Everyone tells Me they did not think about nourishing themselves because they were always too busy with what they were doing.

Tenth meeting

But the real question is, what are they doing? They have nothing to do with Me until they discover what they are made for, besides whatever they know intellectually, or may have already discovered physically.

Lisa: It looks like You are really tired of hearing our explanations, aren't You?

God: An explanation is an explanation, but the truth can be different from an explanation. People do not stop giving physical food to themselves because they are too busy. That is the truth, not an explanation.

Therefore, they take time, alas, too much time to make money and to buy food. They use so much time to prepare the food they want to eat and spend so many hours around their table eating food.

For Me, it looks like the major focus of human beings is food. In the same way, if they really believed in the truth, not in their explanation that they don't have time, they would nourish their inner self, which is the Me living in them.

And, I did think they would naturally make time for that need, because it is the truth, not an explanation.

Lisa: I feel so sorry that we haven't taken seriously that You exist in us, and our concerns have just been the reality of our physical existence instead of the reality of Your existence in us.

God: It is interesting, the moment human beings arrive to the place where I can tell them I am living inside of them, for some reason they seem to feel threatened and negative about this thought, as if they might lose something. And, many times they drive themselves to forget this idea as soon as possible,

in order to maintain what they used to believe to be their true personality.

But what they surely don't realize is, on the contrary, if they don't believe what I offer to them, they will lose whatever level of development they had already achieved.

In the moment they start to reject the reality of My existence in them, which I was so pleased to tell them about, it is like they refuse to put wings on their plane and yet still dream of flying somewhere with that plane.

Lisa: I certainly don't want to be the person that loses all that she has just gained. But do You know, some people here on Earth have promoted the thought that those who believe in You are oppresssed rather than enlightened?

God: Well, that is an excuse that surely has the power to erase the concept of My existence in them.

The reality is, if human beings try to exist without recognizing Me in them, they will not be able to resemble Me. Indeed, they will more closely resemble the beings that you call animals. Yet, I designed human beings with the potential for My nature to develop in them, and in the process they too would benefit by becoming their true mature selves.

Lisa: I feel humbled by Your words. I can see Your perspective is quite different from whatever we can imagine to be the reason we exist.

God: To explain to you the origin of My thought a little bit, I will use the example of someone who wishes to create something to function in a specific way. This person has an idea to begin with, and then he designs an object according to that idea, doesn't he? It would then be strange to see that

Tenth meeting

object he created suddenly respond to him, "I think you created me for your own benefit, so therefore I won't work for you," when we know that the object now has a chance to perform its function based on the purpose for which it was created.

Lisa: Yes, I agree. We create things for certain purposes, and we hope they will fulfill their purpose, not rebel against us.

God: Likewise, if I say to you that I wanted human beings to have a nature that does not disintegrate, then should I not create you with particular characteristics that do not disintegrate? I did that by planting My nature in you. In that way I am guaranteeing that your nature will exist forever.
    But, there is a problem somewhere.

Lisa: What can that be, My God?

God: My problem starts when I want to grow Myself in someone. Let's say I succeed in making this person believe My fetus is in him or her. But then from that moment I am helpless in front of the reality that I cannot develop the fetus by Myself.
    I can only keep trying to communicate with humankind and ask them to respond to their destiny, but I cannot make them choose that destiny. I can only wait for them to choose it.
    Do you think waiting is a problem?

Lisa: I see. Now I can understand why this is a deep emotional issue for You, as it is for me, since I need to accept and believe in that reality and never erase it, and You need to wait for me.

The Rebirth of God and Lisa

God: Lisa, I know it will not always be easy to be aware of My presence in you. Before you, there were many other people who tried to comprehend that element of Me in themselves. They too had immense difficulty to accept and keep the belief in what I brought them to realize. They many times forgot or didn't take this understanding seriously.

Lisa: That makes me question why it's so difficult to accept and to keep believing in Your truth. Is there something in me that has the tendency to reject the reality of Your fetus in me?

God: Yes, absolutely. There is something in you that refuses to accept the Me to grow inside you, regardless that what I teach you is only for the purpose of fulfilling what your heart most desires.

Lisa: I want You to know today that I do like what You tell me. I also want to admit that I have a number of mixed feelings. Some are joyful, but in other ways I feel very nervous. I'm concerned that I will have a hard time to remember to nourish the You in me everyday, because You are too invisible.

God: I see. Regardless of what you say, I would like to add something.

Because I could manifest Myself to you and explain My presence in many different ways, and because in these moments you allowed yourself to listen and to accept these theories, you automatically removed some of the nature of resistance toward My word. This is what we call, 'growing'.

If you can maintain your belief in the understanding I gave you today, it means the nature of resistance in you will continue to be destroyed and it will be replaced by My nature.

This is your task.

Tenth meeting

Lisa: From the time You began to speak to me, even though I perceived a certain resistance every so often, my desire to understand and to accept what You say has become more dominant.

I guess because I agreed with You, this must have changed my nature of rejection.

God: I like it when you are sincere. Because of your sincerity, it is easier for Me to explain everything to you. When someone is sincere, it means that person has already digested what they received, therefore it is easy to give them new food.

Lisa: I will try to stay sincere with You, my God, since this is what pleases You. And, I believe I won't doubt what You say any longer.

God: I think we have spent this time well, Lisa.

Lisa: Thank you, my God.

ELEVENTH MEETING

The Rebirth of God and Lisa

Even though I had much more knowledge about God than I used to, I could also see that having knowledge doesn't necessarily mean we follow what we know. Seeing many discrepancies in myself made me feel unstable and not in control, which was not so easy for someone such as me who likes to have everything under control.

However, except for me, no one could really tell what was going on, since it is easy to cover what is happening inside of us. At my workplace no one realized that I was in the process of redefining myself.

Now, I want to again share with you what God said to me when He came to visit me some time later.

God: As time passes according to the measurement of your clock, I hope You remember Me and also remember what I said to you concerning what is inside of you, which is My seed that demands to be developed.

Lisa: Actually, from time to time I do forget, but everytime I do so, I feel so sad and try to make extra effort to recall Your words.

God: The difficulty you have at your stage of growth is to keep your awareness of something invisible inside you. For example, because you know what a leg looks like, you can

Eleventh meeting

remember it. You have a name for it because it is physical.

On the other hand, I understand it is not easy to keep an awareness of the reality of having a developing fetus that you cannot see with your physical senses. Yet all this doesn't mean the fetus is not inside of you.

Lisa: Yes, it's true, it's not so easy to keep an awareness of Your presence inside me, therefore I can forget to give food to my fetus.

God: Fortunately, I can give you a clue to help you to recognize the presence and the needs of your fetus. Besides your physical feelings of satisfaction or dissatisfaction, there is a specific organ in your body that has the responsibility to tell you the condition of your fetus. However, I think I might have forgotten the name of that organ.

Lisa: What? You can't remember? How is that possible?

God: It was a long time ago that I created that organ. But the worst thing for Me is that earthly people change the names of things every century or so, and sometimes I get confused about which name to use. I constantly need to relearn the language of people before I can explain to them what I want to say.

That is hard work, don't you think?

Lisa: Just thinking You could no longer talk to me in my language makes me feel anxious. You see, when You communicate to me I can feel so many emotions based on Your words.

God: It looks like you start to understand what words are for. They are not just meant to explain something, they also create a receptacle that carries energy. This energy will make a positive effect in your body, if the energy is positive, or a negative effect, if the energy is negative.

Lisa: Yes, I can see that what You say to me is not just knowledge to add to what I already know, but You also create a feeling in me through each word You use. The major reason I like to listen to You is because of the feelings You create in Me and not just because of the information You give to me.

God: Yes, words have the ability to explain something to you, as well as the power to stimulate emotions inside of you. Therefore when you learn to speak, you are learning to communicate emotion as well as knowledge.

So, if you learn language with this view, surely the quality of the words you use to explain things should be valued according to the amount of feelings you produce in the one who listens to you. When you can create a lot of feelings then you can say you are the beginning, and you can say you are a potential creator.

Lisa: Yes, I begin to see what effect language can have, and I want to choose my words carefully. But do You remember, my God, You said there is a special organ that will help me to know what my fetus needs?

God: Oh, yes. I was trying to find the word in your dictionary matching to what I want to say. I think the word I was thinking about is something like 'sciencecon'. Do you understand this word?

Lisa: I don't ever remember hearing that word. Are You sure

Eleventh meeting

that's the right word according to our vocabulary?

God: Oh, I think I've got it backwards! It is not 'sciencecon' but 'conscience'! I have I talked to you about the conscience before, but I don't know if you were aware that it is an organ.

Lisa: Some time ago You talked to me about following what my conscience asked me to do, in order to become a lovely being who will be able to communicate with You for eternity. I thought of it as some voice we hear from time to time, but not as an organ.

God: To explain the conscience in more detail, it is an organ with the capability to receive and to process information, and to pass that information on. To give an example, every time the fetus inside you needs something, it emits some vibration. The conscience picks up this vibration and transforms it into words, which are then received by your brain.

Do you understand now? It is not just some voice, but an organ with the responsibility to convey the wishes of your fetus to you, according to a specific time and place in your growth.

Lisa: Well, it's amazing to have an organ that gives us a way to know what is happening in the deepest part of ourselves.

God: The conscience is similar to the physical organ inside your head that collects information from your senses. If your brain is damaged, you will no longer know where is right or left, or if what you say makes sense. The brain maintains the balance in your secular existence.

In the same way, the conscience maintains the balance of your internal existence. It collects information from your most invisible part and then reveals it to you through your mind, hoping you will listen to it and act upon its direction.

Lisa: It seems that this places a lot of responsibility upon me to be obedient to my conscience, doesn't it?

God: Well, nobody needs to teach you to take responsibility for the way your limbs move, you just take responsibility naturally. The same as you pay attention to how your hands and feet move, you need to take care of everything else existing in you, especially your conscience.

Lisa: I see Your point. If I hear my conscience and refuse to pay attention to it, because at the time I feel what it asks me to do is too demanding, then I understand the consequence can be that I will starve the fetus in me. That's quite serious, isn't it?

God: The way you make your conclusion is quite impressive. Through you I can perceive human beings like to think and put everything together. The only point missing is that after they understand everything, they are not so concerned about following what they know and making everything function the way it is supposed to.

Besides that, it is correct that if your conscience mentions to you that your fetus needs food and you refuse to feed it, because you perhaps feel you need to take it easy or because you feel what you hear is not meant for you, the tragedy is that your fetus will starve, to the point it can die without you even being aware of it.

This is the reason many religious people teach the concept that human beings are dead and need to be resurrected, without maybe realizing fully what they are talking about.

Eleventh meeting

Lisa: Honestly speaking, I never knew how crucial it was to follow what we hear from our conscience. But now, knowing the origin of my conscience, I will try my best to respond to it.

God: Your conscience not only knows that your fetus is in need of food, but also knows what kind of food is necessary at specific moments in the development of your inner being.

Throughout My existence I have experienced vividly what human beings look like when they don't follow their conscience, to the point I regretted creating them. But because a few could begin to recognize their conscience, then I started to feel interested in human beings again. But still, it was not enough to make Me happy.

I can tell you, only when human beings acknowledge their conscience as the organ that shows them the deepest part of themselves, and only when they can accept to be raised to maturity by following its direction, then I will feel they are the most majestic creation from amongst all things whose creation I initiated.

Lisa: I see. It looks like we human beings understand many things, but we miss what is most important, and after all, we understand very little. If I could look from Your perspective, I believe You must think we understand nothing.

God: When human beings accept My existence, it should not be difficult for them to understand that I am the One who gives nourishment to their inner selves as well. Then, if human beings would turn to Me, over and over, they would receive My nourishment, which they call 'love', for their fetuses. But without that love, the fetus will be incapable of growing, and will therefore stay dormant inside of them, to the point I will consider Myself as not having created these human beings.

Lisa: So regardless we believe in this fetus, if we don't receive Your nourishment for it, can we consider that we have not yet been born?

God: Yes, you understand well now. I guess it is simple after I explain it. So far, human beings haven't seemed to comprehend the function of the conscience. At different times there have been people who said they wanted to follow their conscience, which made Me excited in that moment, to the point I wanted to meet them. But then they stopped listening to their conscience, and because of that I saw them changing directions, going opposite to the place where I was expecting we could meet together. Surely it was a miserable situation, because all My dreams were destroyed.

Lisa: I'm very sorry. I think we have never been able to imagine Your situation. For us, just to believe in our conscience is still a big question for us.

But to imagine that You expect us to grow Your fetus within us is truly another dimension.

God: In your world, when someone creates an object, he usually also creates a name for that object and for each part of that object, in order to be able to identify each piece in case something doesn't go well. If the names don't match to the pieces then confusion begins, and no one will be able to use those pieces to produce something positive, or to be able to fix that object if something stops working.

Since human beings do not have the right words and definitions concerning what is happening inside of them, it is extremely difficult to check the reality of their situation. So, until your people define themselves well, they will be unable to develop themselves.

Eleventh meeting

Lisa: I understand very well what You are saying. Many times, when I watch a show on television or read a book that explains how people function mentally or emotionally, I feel confused by all the words that different so-called experts use. It seems the meanings of the words change according to the expert. This is the reason I prefer to learn about fields where words mean what they mean and don't change according to someone's opinion.

God: It is indeed difficult to function well if you don't understand what each part is to be used for. Now do you understand what the conscience is for? It is made to perceive what is happening in the deepest part of your existence.

Lisa: It seems so simple that it's hard to believe this is it. You see, we have a tendency here to believe that what is simple cannot be true, or that it is childish. Instead, what looks complex has a tendency to be labeled as being true.

God: Well, it is similar to having pain in an area of your body but not having knowledge about your different organs. What will happen is, you will continue to have pain until someone who knows about the different organs can discover the cause of the pain, in your stomach, for example. Then perhaps you can learn that when a stomach is empty, or trying to digest something that doesn't break down easily, it produces a certain chemical reaction that can be perceived as pain. Of course, you can say to Me that this is really simple knowledge, but when did human beings discover these things? Do you know?

Therefore, it is similar to people who have tried to identify the pain in the deepest part of themselves, which you now know is their conscience screaming that My fetus inside them needs to be nourished. So surely, knowledge does have great

value in helping human beings to fulfill their potential.

Lisa: I'm very grateful for Your explanation, my God.

God: Yes indeed, Lisa. The course of history is a difficult one because human beings have so little patience to be educated by Me. And, even if they do receive some knowledge, they have so little loyalty toward My viewpoint. Therefore, they are predestined or condemned to be unable to receive the elements of life for their fetuses.

As you know, if you cannot receive nourishment for the miniature Me inside of you, you will start to hear a voice bursting out from within yourself saying that you are not complete, and you will never feel satisfied. This pain can become so high it can turn into anger. It is similar to a person with nothing inside his stomach. He might even kill someone else in order to satisfy his pain.

Lisa: I'm a bit shocked to hear that such extreme anger can come from the fact that we lack the nourishment requested by our innermost selves.

God: You are shocked? I am tired of perceiving this reality, over and over. If human beings would only choose to take the road of turning humbly to Me, it would be possible for them to fulfill the longing of their hearts and to grow the Me inside them. Instead, they choose another road that makes them try all kinds of things to satisfy their needs. This road can even bring them to the extreme stage of destroying their bodies, believing they will finally have peace and be relieved of their internal pain.

Lisa: When You tell me about joyful situations, I feel

Eleventh meeting

weightless. But when You talk to me about tragic situations that happened to human beings or to You, even though You say only a few words, I start to feel very heavy.

God: When the voice of the conscience starts to bother your people, they will often use other sounds for the purpose of making it impossible to hear their conscience. They will either create sounds by talking louder than the conscience that is calling them, or they will turn to other devices that produce noise around them.

But, if I may ask you, what do you think about a mother who turns the music or the television up louder in order to not hear the cries of her child?

Lisa: Oh, I see! Actually, I did make noise for many years. Then at some point I began to feel tired of the noise around me. I somehow realized it was covering up feelings inside of me, as You have described so well.

God: If human beings had not learned to starve their fetuses, no human being would turn out to be deformed or, from your angle, look strange or bizarre. As well, humans would not have practiced such an enormous amount of violent techniques, whose purpose was to attack the most sensitive part of themselves and others. It is only by growing this sensitive part that human beings can fulfill their harmonious destiny, at which point they would be incapable of violence against each other.

Tragically, their perpetual attacks against this most sensitive part have stopped them from discovering the beauty and majesty of their inner nature, which is actually the combination of Me with their noble self.

Lisa: From Your viewpoint we must look barbaric and brutal.

God: I do not know the words to describe someone who doesn't want to nurture something so graceful, gentle and fragile inside of himself or herself. It is difficult for Me to identify such a person as being lovely or caring. This person has a nature very much opposite to the nature of a peacemaker.

Lisa: After Your explanation and seeing what I did to myself, I surely cannot use the word 'lovely' for myself. I can only agree with You that we are not peaceful beings, but instead we are beings who are violent to the highest degree.

God: To go back to the point where we began our conversation, about your conscience being the voice of your fetus asking for nourishment, I want to add that you are coming to a stage where you will hear that voice often. You will need to take care of your fetus as often as the voice demands, because it is in the most vulnerable stage of its creation as your future original being. Therefore your support is crucial until that fetus, who is now being born, can receive love naturally, like breathing in and out.

Lisa: I would like to ask You, my God, does every human being have You inside of him or herself?

God: Well Lisa, to answer you, I want to use the example of a walnut tree. There are several stages in its growth. First come the trunk, branches and leaves, and then after it has reached a certain stage of maturity the tree produces blooms that grow into fruits, which are the walnuts. A walnut is both a fruit and a seed, which is the beginning of another tree.

Eleventh meeting

Lisa: Yes, I see.

God: Similarly, within yourself, I may be existing as a concept or a belief, which is comparable to growing the trunk, branches, and leaves, but You only start to perceive Me from the moment you begin to produce fruit. At this point, the seed of your internal self, or your eternal being, begins to grow. Now you will begin to notice the demands of the seed inside you, which is My heart inside you asking you to grow your love.

Lisa: Yes, I start to feel Your heart inside me asking many things.

God: Yes, Lisa, if you compare yourself to a tree that is still in the process of growing its trunk and branches, then you, Lisa, are extremely lucky to be at the stage where your conscience is demanding you to resemble Me in the most lovely way.

Lisa: You want to say, my God, that although this stage feels difficult right now, it means that I'm approaching the fulfillment of my destiny, which is to resemble You?

God: All human beings are responsible to grow their tree to the stage where it is able to produce a flower, which can then turn into a fruit. At this most delicate stage they need to keep their fruit on the tree until it can become mature.
    Becoming mature depends on whether or not each individual pursues the desire to develop him or herself to the highest degree. If people allow themselves to grow until they can recognize My seed inside of them, they will at the same time see a new birth, the birth of their heart, taking place in them. At that moment they will surely know they are created by Me and through Me.

Lisa: If I look at my life based on what You reveal to me, I realize the meaning of my physical life is extremely different from what I believed before. I can also see it is quite different from the theory of salvation that is taught here. We definitely don't know about this concept of Your seed growing inside of us.

God: I do not know your theory of salvation, but I do know how I created everything. Anything that is not based on My method of creation cannot produce a mature fruit with seeds.

What I can tell you for sure is that your physical life was meant to protect your inner or your eternal self, who is the Me in you, like a cocoon protects the developing butterfly inside. Through your participation in developing this self to its highest level of maturity, you will produce a being who is qualified to be called a 'true child' by Me, and qualified to be called a lovely person by the people around you.

Lisa: I really want to be qualified to be Your true child!

God: Yes, Lisa. You begin to see My hope for you. If your mind and body were not made to help you grow your inner self, why then should I have created them? Why did I make human beings with such longevity and such importance in this physical world? The only reason is because human beings are destined to grow their inner selves, therefore they need a resistant body that can live for many years, as well as an alert mind. Based on the conjunction of your body and mind, you can receive My energy, which you need during the time you are developing your inner self to the level of maturity.

Unless human beings can achieve that, they are not yet born from My point of view.

Eleventh meeting

Lisa: I'm afraid many people will not really understand what You are talking about. Personally, I want You to grow inside me because I've discovered that my heart is not content. But I believe that those who haven't yet discovered they have a heart will not easily agree that they are not yet born, nor wish to concentrate on developing their inner self.

God: I think it is not so complicated to accept what human beings are made for. When a farmer prepares the land for sowing, does he only need to put the seeds in the land in order to have a good crop? No. He needs to prepare the land beforehand, and after planting the seeds he needs to make sure the new plants are able to resist all kinds of obstacles in order to be harvested one day.

If human beings are happy about having their own land, which they call their body, they also need to question what is supposed to be planted in their body, and what they need to do to cultivate it.

Lisa: You have such a natural way of explaining things. It's true that to guarantee a good harvest, the farmer needs not only to plant the seeds but also to nourish the seedlings. He can't just leave everything to Mother Nature.

God: Since you like My way of explaining things, I now have a question for you. Why do people question the reason they were born, when they are already born physically?

Lisa: To be honest with You, God, I prefer when You give me answers instead of questioning me.

God: Well, your people always question where they come from and why they are on this Earth. Isn't this proof that they did not yet give birth to themselves internally? As well, since they have not yet experienced the birth of Me in themselves, they don't seek to relate with Me.

But if they find a way to be born, then they can focus on growing their inner self to become an adult fruit. And if they achieve that, do you think they will have questions in their heads about their existence any longer?

Instead, they will only be concerned about how to create a relationship with Me and maintain it today, tomorrow and for eternity.

Lisa: Yes, it seems life will become so simple when we start to achieve this. But still, I feel it is a high and far-away goal.

God: If you want to reach a goal in your life, should the vision you have be small and reach only as far as your feet can take you, or should it be big and aimed high as your head is high? Truthfully, human beings are made to always strive for something higher. Based on that, I educate you so you can always try to reach something greater, and not just be satisfied with what you have already achieved.

I also want to say to you, this goal is something to strive for, and not something to be used to judge yourself or to make you feel bad. If you accept to carry the dream I open to you and challenge yourself to fulfill it, you will come to the point where not only are you able to feel I am in you, but I will also feel you are in Me, which will surely make Me experience a new birth as well.

Lisa: Are You are saying that both of us, You and me, will be born at the same time?

God: Yes, absolutely, as incredible as it may sound. Are you

Eleventh meeting

uncomfortable hearing that I also can be born, at the same time as your true self is born?

Lisa: Honestly speaking, I feel awed by what You are saying to me.

God: So, now you know how much value you have for Me. You are born physically to fulfill the destiny of your fetus, to nourish it to grow and to become an adult, before your body surrenders to natural law.

Lisa: I hope I can fulfill what You created me to be. Through what You say I do see why our flesh has so much importance. Maybe this is why people put so much value on the length of their physical lives, regardless they haven't yet found their true purpose.

God: I don't think it is so difficult to become a mature adult being, since I didn't plan that it should be difficult. What you have to remember is to accept to hear the voice of your conscience, knowing it is the voice of your fetus, or the Me in you, demanding food, or love. Receiving the nourishment of love through relating with your Father will enable you to grow to the point where you will be happy to be who you are.

What I am most concerned about when I look at you now is, are you going to continue to turn to Me to receive My love, until the baby God in you can become the teenage God and develop further into the adult God?

If you can do so, it will be your greatest achievement, which will permit Me to truly call you 'My godly daughter'.

Lisa: Oh! What You say is so incredible, I think no one will be able to believe me!

God: The moment you realize I am living in you as a Child and you accept to grow the Me in you to the stage where My heart in you can become the heart of a parent, I will say that you are the most incredible woman of your time.

On the other hand, if you reject the responsibility to grow the Me in you, then you will be just an intelligent woman, but you will never know My heart.

Lisa: I believe now, if I don't mature my heart, You will not be able to make Your heart visible through me, and You will therefore continue to be invisible. This is maybe the reason I stopped believing in You at some point, because I never found anyone with Your heart inside of them.

God: In the history of human beings, people have discovered who I am according to how much they were able to develop their own selves and recognize the Me inside of them. For example, when human beings discovered the world of intelligence, they discovered that I, God, was smart also. At that time they believed their intellect was coming from Me, and started to look at Me as a highly intelligent Being.

But because human beings do not yet value the feelings of their inner selves, or consider these feelings as being My heart, I am for them still the God who has almost no heart and no nature of goodness. This is the reason they usually feel the right to accuse Me of not caring for them, or not loving them.

Due to this reality of human beings, they conclude through their logic that I am, like them, heartless.

Lisa: I now believe that if I accept to recognize my heart as Your heart and grow the You in me, this can end Your misery of being misunderstood. At least I understand that.

Eleventh meeting

God: Throughout My existence, I did have some Sons who fulfilled the destiny of their hearts, but when they revealed their secret to the people around them, they were rejected.

What was special about those Sons was that when they arrived to the place where they discovered that their heart was My heart, they did not reject the concept but instead embraced it and accepted to nourish the Me in them. And, because of this, they revived the dream of My heart for those short moments of time when they were living in the midst of the people. Therefore, I still cannot forget them.

Maybe you know one of My Sons. His name is Jesus.

Lisa: I'm shaking as I listen to You and I feel tears inside myself. I am shocked to hear that what made Jesus so special is because he accepted his heart was Your heart, and therefore he made You his Father.

God: He is extremely special for Me, because he was able to figure out how to develop the Me in him and to reach Me. His only dream was about that. He spoke about Me whenever he addressed the people around him. He could talk about Me over and over because He did become My Son. And, because of who he became, many humans have believed in him at some point in their lives.

Lisa: Oh, I feel so humbled by what You are saying to me!

God: It looks like I have spoken about many things to you this time, haven't I, Lisa?

Lisa: Yes, My God, You have really spoken to my deepest part. I want to say thank you for having so much patience in explaining everything to me during this long conversation.

Now, I wish and hope more than anything else that I can become Your Daughter, as Jesus is Your Son.

God: If I may add something, in the moment you reach adulthood and can say you are My Daughter, the relationship between you and Me will be assured, for that day and for eternity. As My Son used to say, what you seal on Earth will be sealed in Heaven, but what is not sealed yet, has to be sealed.

Lisa: I can feel our conversation is drawing to an end for now, which is emotionally difficult for me. I feel so different when You are not here in the way You are now. But I want to say thank You to come to visit Me so many times, and I fervently hope to grow myself so that You can feel happy when You come again.

God: Before I leave you, as you already have perceived, I want to say to you that what you give birth to on Earth, you also give birth to in Heaven. What you grow and develop on Earth remains forever. What you create on Earth will be part of you today and tomorrow. What you love will be part of you as long as you exist.

Through all these processes, you will become the Me in you. You will be the place for Me to dwell so we can become One, for eternity.

Lisa: Thank You, my Father. I love You.

TWELFTH MEETING

Notes from Lisa

Since my last conversation with God, I have continued to nourish the relationship with the fetus of God in me. To each of you who has been traveling with me on this journey, it is my highest hope that you have also discovered your own fetus of God growing within you. I also hope that you will listen to the inner voice that reveals to you where and how to find nourishment.

I feel that the meaning of this final meeting is forever unfolding, beginning with your own conversation with God in you. The following pages are left open for you to write down your experiences along your journey to meet God.

Each time I reread my journal I discover something deeper and each time I turn to Him I feel something richer growing inside of me. I hope you can have the same experience and can welcome this invitation for each of us to become God's own Sons and Daughters.

Twelfth meeting

 The Rebirth of God and Lisa

Twelfth meeting

www.ingramcontent.com/pod-product-compliance
Lightning Source LLC
LaVergne TN
LVHW051551070426
835507LV00021B/2526